ALWAYS CRASHING

ISSUE THREE

CHICAGO, ILLINOIS • PITTSBURGH, PENNSYLVANIA

ISBN: 978-0-578-68902-9

Always Crashing is a magazine of fiction, poetry, and nameless things around and in-between. We publish one print issue per year and feature online content year-round. We are headquartered in Chicago, Illinois, and Pittsburgh, Pennsylvania.

Editors: Jessica Berger & James Tadd Adcox

Managing Editor: Helenmary Sheridan

The editors wish to thank Matthew Kosinski, Gesina Phillips, Emily Kiernan, and Elayne Sheridan for their generous support.

Always Crashing is reader supported: we do not charge submission fees from writers, and we receive no institutional support. If you'd like to find out more about supporting *Always Crashing*, please visit our Patreon page: www.patreon.com/alwayscrashingmag

For submission guidelines, ordering information, and access to our electronic edition featuring new work every two weeks, please visit www.alwayscrashing.com

SIDE A

SIDE B

/ side a

BLANK SUN SONNET

/ Joanna Cleary

Today I ran hard into the sun, burn
　ing up in Apollo's fleshy hands be
　　cause the immortal red of his wounds sur
　　tured themselves before they could begin re
　　leasing me; I died from inside a blem
　　ished god; I died an explorer secret
　　ly wanting to write everyone I al
　　ways planned to forgive one day sonnets un
　rhyming their way back to me so my love
　rs could unlove and my mothers could be
come the light I must now walk slowly to
wards as I approach my father's drumbeat
ing heart, its chambers celibate with mort
al blood, a land where shadows fade to myth

TRIPTYCH OF FEVER DREAM W/ INTERIOR EXISTENCE

/ Nicholas Alti

[1] – <u>A BRIEF OVERVIEW ON THE CURRENT STATE OF THINGS</u>

i typically take two tries to put on a shirt right
i think i'm fucked up as a human being

    as a burnout most of my shit is burnt & ash ridden & as a specter
        you might not see me depleting but i dilute continuously

                really what i need is bottomless
mimosas   indefinitely

    i'm mostly art-deco but also useless in general like an ornate mask
for an anonymous orgy but you're wasted & it fell off without your noticing &
you're just doing the most wild shit ever, thinking *no problem i'm good* but you're so not good

    something delicate that falters & ruins itself

i steal stuff from my friends   toilet paper mostly, hats, screwdrivers, lighters, condoms

maybe that's just my thing   be a complete piece of shit always

[2] – <u>AS AN ADULT WITH FEW DECENT PROSPECTS, MY PLAN FOR THE FUTURE</u>

           i haven't gotten arrested in a few years, but
(& this is between us)

        i'm thinking of robbing a rehab

one of those really nice ones with Palominos & mints on a beach littered with jellyfish carcasses

they'll all be too zombified & unaware in withdrawals to stop me

& y'all know those employees don't give a fuck about a junky so they won't try to stop me

i mean i'm a junky & i don't even give a fuck about rich junkies & besides
what do they need? *i* need   i should probably also sit in on a few meetings

        after all, might as well two kill stones with one birds
                                sorry i'm killed as stones right now   i'm like, thirty birds
no i'm two stoned birds wearing lipstick
                                        SQUAWK!! hah no i'm kidding that was weird
                                usually i'm great in these situations   a real laugh riot

hey at least i think i'm funny
hey at least i think   maybe
hey at least   i'm   shit

look usually i'm not so apathetic usually i'm happily drunk on Bellinis & other southern luxuries

we could all agree to catapult me to Orion yes but honestly just let me use your toothbrush dude

i mean i know i'm not perfect but do we really need to consider banishing me from this orbit

oh wait what's that? that's not what we're talking about?   yeah now that you mention it
                                                i don't know who you are either
        hey sorry bro my bad but seriously do you have any extra cash or weed?

[3] – <u>I EXIST ALWAYS FRIGHTENED SOMETHING WILL GROW AGAIN IN MY
BRAIN TO DEBILATTE MY BEING THEREFORE MUST QUELL THE EXTER-
NAL THREAT BY RECLAIMING AUTONOMY IN THE ACT OF SELF-DECON-
STRUCTION</u>

                once, my face was mostly removed

                                        i was a rosebud beneath myself

this *Reservoir Dogs* style team of crackpot mercenary surgeons had to remove a growing tumor
although it left its insidious remnants

usually when i tell people i got my skull cracked open & brain made cartography by a scalpel

(SUPER traumatic for a child by the way)

they're like "oh that explains it LOL!"   or "makes sense LOL!"

or "hey man give me some space who are you" which is understandable
cause this is a pretty big park & it's like two a.m. but still not very sympathetic???

basically i learned early that to fix myself   (for i am & long have been utterly broken)

destroy away

    for health i need dismantling

now i can sever anything

as if i'm some large worm

a body might numb before giving & that is an apex in itself

GIRLHOOD I-III

/ Emily Barton Altman

Girlhood I

>Steal a building.
>Place yourself
>in its halls after dark.

Girlhood II

>Steal an architecture.
>Place yourself
>in a city.

Girlhood III

>Steal a constellation.
>Place yourself
>in the sky.

MORNING I-III

/ Emily Barton Altman

Morning I

    survey your house

Morning II

    consume its memory

Morning III

    collapse the house and curate the ashes

A CONDITION...

/ Armand Eduard

TWICE RABBITS

/ Armand Eduard

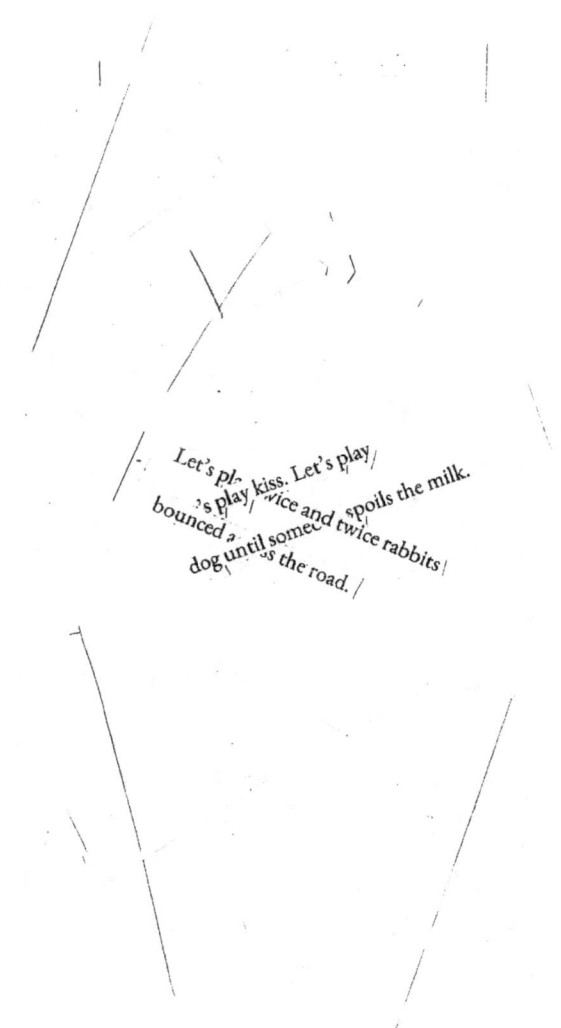

Let's pl~ kiss. Let's play
's play/ 'vice and spoils the milk.
bounced a ... twice rabbits/
dog until somet ...s the road. /

AT LEAST

/ Armand Eduard

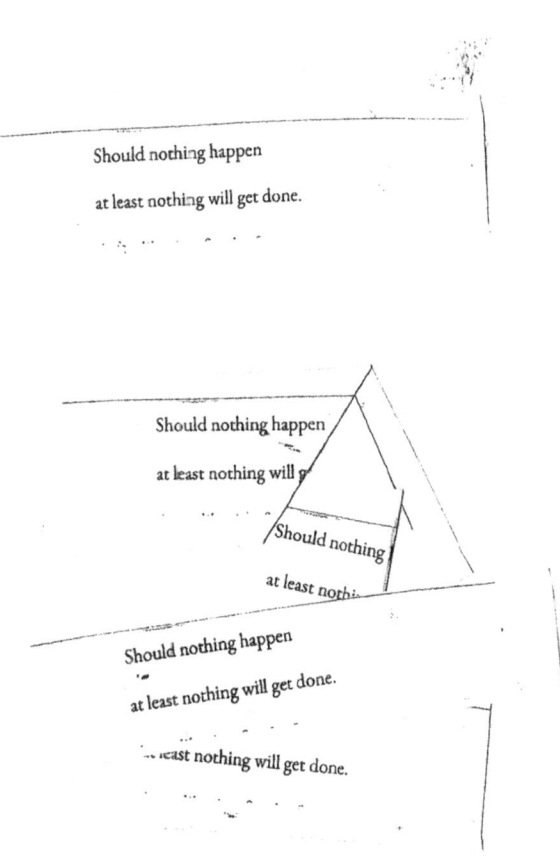

Should nothing happen

at least nothing will get done.

ASTRALPROJECT

/ Rob Wilson Engle

this is not my life   this is a methodology   for
redaction   I've been known to hurt people
using my body   then taking it away   the day
I am seized   by a tide of blue rapture   is when
I'll be comfortable   in submission   sadness
deviates itself   from the bone map of my body
when you move
                me
            around in slow   uneven
                                        circles
like rum when you're young   then you spend the
rest of your life   becoming a serious animal
the owner of   a little wooden box   that you
live in   and walk around its little different rooms
you pay insurance   and prepare yourself   a nice
steak dinner   every Monday   trying not to
occupy   the nearest vessel   when all of a sudden

                    ::

you find yourself in the wet gaping mouth of April
in a house where   too many people love you
everything's embarrassing   and you are of average
intelligence   parallelograms of sunlight stretch
into your bed   as someone stretches out of it   a
catfish   visited your dream last night   *all of this*
is hypothetical   he said in his catfish-tongue
before swimming away   that same moment you
reached for your teeth   and instead found a song

                    ::

a beam of light   a rose   a specter
at some point   you've wrapped into yourself
learned the feeling   of becoming soft   without
the consequence   of shame   the way an arm
can reach straight through your shadow   to the
other wall   and turn off the light

SORRY I WASN'T AT YOUR PARTY

/ Rob Wilson Engle

I was busy thinking what it's like to catch fire   what
when   the wind contributes   to your state
of panic   makes you regret   not waking up
thinking about God   and thanking him that
you are not dead   or a match   & maybe
in another life   you'll be   a cactus in the valley
limbs skywards in adoration   you've received
just enough manna   but not much   enough
to make   your head explode   into a rose

sing praise   sing praise

THE SMOKE-FILLED ROOM (#29)

/ Colin Rafferty

It's all out of your hands now. ~ ~ ~ ~ ~ ~ ~ ~ ~ ~ ~ ~ ~ ~ ~ ~
~ ~
~ ~
~ ~
~ ~
~ ~
~ ~
~ ~
~ ~
~ ~
~ From a room
in Chicago's Blackstone Hotel, the decision comes forth. You, War-
ren G. Harding, Ohio's son: you will be the candidate; you will be
the president. ~
~ ~
~ ~
~ ~
~ ~
~ ~
~ ~
~ ~ ~ ~ ~ ~ The cigars burn in the smoke-filled room. You can see
the ashes glow, the cherry, it's called. The men regard you. They ask
you if there's anything lurking in the closet. Anything they should
know. You think of Florence. You think of Nan. The other girls. ~ ~
~ ~
~ ~
~ ~
~ ~
~ ~
~ ~
~ ~ ~ ~ ~ ~ ~ ~ ~ ~ ~ ~ ~ ~ ~ ~ ~ ~ ~ *No*, you say. It's your
one moment of agency, that lie. That's all. Nothing else. ~ ~ ~ ~ ~

~ ~
~ ~
~ ~
~ ~
~ ~
~ ~
~ ~
~ ~
~ ~
~ ~

~ ~ ~ ~ ~ The men in the smoke-filled room nod. You are now the candidate. The next ballot of the convention, the tenth, the stalemate breaks. Florence, your wife, is so surprised she accidentally jabs your political manager with a hatpin. ~ ~ ~ ~ ~ ~ ~ ~ ~ ~
~ ~
~ ~
~ ~
~ ~
~ ~
~ ~

The managers. You are managed. Your job for the campaign is to give speeches from your front porch. The managers will do the rest. ~ ~
~ ~
~ ~
~ ~
~ ~
~ ~
~ ~
~ ~
~ ~
~ ~

~ ~ ~ ~ ~ ~ ~ ~ They'll film you (new technology) and send the footage to the newsreels. ~ ~ ~ ~ ~ ~ ~ ~ ~ ~ ~ ~ ~ ~ ~ ~ ~ ~
~ ~
~ ~
~ ~
~ ~

~ ~
~ ~
~ ~
~ ~They'll
bring celebrities (new tactics) to the front porch and photograph
you with them, 8,000 photos of you and Florence every two weeks.
~ ~
~ ~
~ ~
~ ~
~ ~
~ ~They'll train speak-
ers to go around the country and talk to people about you. 5,000
speakers, 2,000 of them female (new voting block). ~ ~ ~ ~ ~ ~ ~
~ ~
~ ~
~ ~
~ ~
~ ~
~ ~
~ ~
~ ~ ~ ~ ~ ~ ~ ~ ~They'll telephone people (new technology) at
their homes, call them, tell them *vote for Harding*, tell them *return to
normalcy*. ~
~ ~
~ ~
~ ~
~ ~
~ ~
~ ~They'll help
them forget the war, Mr. Wilson's war, *over there*, the trenches, the
gas, the boys who didn't come home, the ones who did, shell-
shocked, faces and bodies destroyed: that's all over for the public
You're the man, they say, to return us to normalcy. ~ ~ ~ ~ ~ ~ ~ ~
~ ~
~ ~
~ ~

~ ~
~ ~
~ ~
~ ~ ~ ~ ~ ~ ~ ~ ~ ~ ~ ~ You'll never go back to normalcy.
When you step off the wood of that porch to go to Washington, your
feet will never touch it again. ~ ~ ~ ~ ~ ~ ~ ~ ~ ~ ~ ~ ~ ~ ~ ~ ~
~ ~
~ ~
~ ~
~ ~
~ ~
~ ~
~ ~
~ ~
~ ~Your image is
out of your hands. Your voice on the recordings is out of your hands.
~ ~
~ ~
~ ~
~ ~
~ ~
~ ~
~ ~
~ ~
~ ~
~ ~ ~ ~ ~ ~ ~ ~ ~ ~ Even this second person point of view, this
reference to Warren Gamaliel Harding, 29th President of the Unit-
ed States of America as *you*, it's a ruse, a writer's tactic perpetrated
by Colin Rafferty, the author of this essay, one of a series of forty-six
about the presidents. It's a trick done in the hopes of getting you
(the reader) to relate to *you* (Warren Harding), dead all these years,
a pathetic president, a joke of a chief executive if he's remembered
at all. ~
~ ~
~ ~
~ ~
~ ~

~ ~
~ An attempt to
close the gap. Open the door. Air out the room. ~ ~ ~ ~ ~ ~ ~ ~
~ ~
~ ~
~ ~
~ ~
~ ~
~ ~
~ ~
~ ~
~ ~
~ ~ ~ ~ It doesn't work. You're elected. They take over. ~ ~ ~ ~ ~
~ ~
~ ~
~ ~
~ ~
~ ~
~ ~
~ ~
~ ~
~ ~
~ ~ ~ ~ ~ ~ They make the decisions. They issue the contracts.
They find a little place called Teapot Dome and make it a synonym
for scandal. They take the Justice Department, the Shipping Board,
and the Veterans Bureau and fill their own coffers from them. ~ ~
~ ~
~ ~
~ ~
~ ~
~ (The Vet-
erans Bureau, too, so soon after the war, with all those veterans to
help.) ~
~ ~
~ ~
~ ~
~ ~

~ ~ ~ ~ ~ ~ ~ ~ ~ ~ ~ ~ ~ ~ ~ They're a gang. You're nothing. You live in the White House. They meet in a green house on K Street and plan their riches. From the Blackstone Hotel to here. From the Blackstone Hotel to there. ~ ~ ~ ~ ~ ~ ~ ~ ~ ~ ~ ~ ~ ~ ~ ~ ~ ~
~ ~
~ ~
~ ~
~ ~
~ ~
~ ~
~ ~ ~ ~ You say to William Allen White, *I have no trouble with my enemies, but my damn friends, they're the ones that keep me walking the floor nights!* ~
~ ~
~ ~
~ ~
~ ~
~ ~
~ ~
~ ~
~ ~
~ ~ ~ ~ ~ ~ ~ ~ ~ ~ ~ ~ It's the most famous thing you say. ~
~ ~
~ ~
~ ~
~ ~
~ ~
~ ~
~ ~
~ ~
~ ~ ~ ~ ~ ~ ~ ~ ~ Passive voice, Warren G. Harding. You are done to. You are undone. You are literally the second person, the one not in charge, the one removed. You are lost in this place, this smoke-filled room, this sea of text, approximately equal. ~ ~ ~ ~
~ ~
~ ~

~ ~
~ ~
~ ~
~ ~
~ ~
~ ~
~ ~ ~ ~ ~ ~ ~ ~ ~ ~ ~ But you know enough to know that in
America, you go west to escape. ~ ~ ~ ~ ~ ~ ~ ~ ~ ~ ~ ~ ~ ~ ~
~ ~
~ ~
~ ~
~ ~
~ ~
~ ~
~ ~
~ ~
~ Ohio was
once the frontier, your front porch a wilderness. So you go west. ~
~ ~
~ ~
~ ~
~ ~
~ ~
~ ~
~ ~
~ ~
~ ~
~ ~
~ ~
~ ~
~ ~
~ ~
~ ~
~ ~ ~ ~ First to Saint Louis, then Kansas, Denver, Tacoma. Then to

Alaska and Canada, first president to do so. You give a speech to fifty thousand in Vancouver, amplified by microphones. ~ ~ ~ ~ ~
~ ~
~ ~
~ ~
~ ~
~ ~
~ ~
~ ~ ~ ~ ~ (new technology) ~ ~ ~ ~ ~ ~ ~ ~ ~ ~ ~ ~ ~ ~
~ ~
~ ~
~ ~
~ ~ ~ ~ ~ ~ ~ ~ ~ ~ ~ You are far from the front porch, from the smoke-filled room. ~ ~ ~ ~ ~ ~ ~ ~ ~ ~ ~ ~ ~ ~ ~ ~ ~ ~ ~
~ ~
~ ~
~ ~
~ ~
~ ~
~ ~ ~ ~ Are you your own man? You are weaker without them, without the men in the smoke-filled room. Never forget: they do. You are done to. ~
~ ~
~ ~
~ ~
~ ~
~ ~
~ ~
~ ~
~ ~
~ ~
~ ~
~ ~
~ ~
~ ~
~ ~ ~ ~ ~ ~ ~ ~ ~ ~ ~ ~ ~ ~ ~ You are done for. ~ ~ ~ ~ ~ ~

~ ~
~ ~
~ ~
~ ~
~ ~
~ ~
~ ~
~ ~
~ ~
~ ~

~ ~ ~ ~ ~ ~ ~ ~ ~ In San Francisco, your heart gives out. In the terror of it, in the shooting pains down the left arm which no one pays attention to, in the misdiagnosis a week earlier of food poisoning, in those final moments of your life, a life of affability and malleability, do you feel the smallest bit of relief? ~ ~ ~ ~ ~ ~ ~ ~ ~ ~

~ ~
~ ~
~ ~
~ ~
~ ~
~ ~
~ ~
~ ~
~ ~
~ ~

~ Today, you're ranked near the bottom. You, Nixon, Grant, Andrew Johnson. The corruptible. I'm sorry. It may not be your fault You were, if nothing else, a pleasant man, someone with whom to pass the time on the front porch. ~ ~ ~ ~ ~ ~ ~ ~ ~ ~ ~ ~ ~ ~ ~

~ ~
~ ~
~ ~
~ ~
~ ~
~ ~
~ ~
~ ~

~ Relief seems a ridiculous notion. Perhaps in those final moments, you thought of Florence, of Nan, of new technology, of new tactics,

of an author years in the future. Maybe the moment when they brought you into the smoke-filled room, the moment before the moment that mattered, and asked you about yourself. ~ ~ ~ ~ ~
~ ~
~ ~
~ ~
~ ~
~ ~ ~ ~ ~ ~ ~ ~ ~ ~ ~ ~ ~ ~ ~~ ~ ~ ~ ~ ~ ~ ~ ~ ~ ~ ~ ~
~ ~
~ ~

~ ~ ~ ~ ~ ~ ~ ~ Go ahead, imagine it: a moment in which you might have said *yes. I have secrets.* ~ ~ ~ ~ ~ ~ ~ ~ ~ ~ ~ ~ ~ ~ ~
~ ~
~ ~
~ ~
~ ~
~ ~
~ ~
~ ~
~ ~
~ ~
~ ~
~ ~
~ ~
~ ~

~ ~ ~ ~ ~ ~ ~ ~ ~ ~ ~ ~ ~ ~ ~ ~ ~ ~ *They cannot be taken from me.* ~
~ ~
~ ~
~ ~
~ ~
~ ~
~ ~
~ ~
~ ~

Name:_____   Date: _____

WHAT THE FUCK HAPPENED LAST NIGHT?: A POP QUIZ

/ Marisa Crane

Directions: Read each question carefully then choose the corresponding answer. You are permitted to use any clues you may have found while cleaning up this morning. You can have as long as you need to complete the quiz but ideally, I'd like to hear back from you ASAP so I can stop sweating all over Jamie's couch, where I currently sit drinking boxed wine and talking like a turnstile. Don't get me wrong, she's rather excited about the whole ordeal—this is crazy "even for you," she says—but as you can imagine, she will soon grow tired of lying to me that everything's going to be okay. Don't worry if you fail the quiz—there was no imaginable way to prepare for something like this.

True or False: ½ point each

Please write either T or F next to each of the following statements. If you don't know or don't remember, leave it blank. Beware: I can read people, even through notebook paper. Hopefully you can too. Then you'll know that I want to turn my skin inside out. That I want to stop throwing up in Jamie's shower long enough to slip some acid under my tongue. That I want to hold my life up to the light and see what I'm made of.

1. You understand the gravity of the situation we are in.

2. You, too, are profoundly hungover.

3. Your panic attacks are having panic attacks.

4. You keep replaying the random scenes you can remember: your arms around my neck, my necklace breaking, my body moving on top of yours.

5. You have been with a woman prior to last night.

6. You knew what was going to happen when you invited me over for Old Fashioneds.

7. We broke apart before your husband made it to the bottom of the stairs.

8. Your husband paid for my cab home.

9. You are pretending that last night didn't happen.

10. You felt the tectonic plates of your world shift beneath you this morning.

11. You are drinking again.

12. Your kids want to know when I'll come over and play with them again.

13. You have feelings for me.

14. You want me to want you to have feelings for me.

15. Your hand is shaking worse than mine.

16. In an alternate universe, you leave him and we run away together.

17. In this universe, you leave him and we run away together.

18. This will happen again.

19. We made a huge mistake.

20. You felt it too when we first met—the pull.

21. Your husband doesn't satisfy you.

22. This is simply a case of falling for the forbidden.

23. I am nothing more than a fun escape from your mundane reality.

24. I'm an asshole for suggesting the above.

25. You keep typing then erasing, typing then erasing.

26. You want to rip this quiz up and eat it.

27. You've never felt anything this intense and it terrifies you.

28. We were doomed from the start.

Multiple Choice: 1 point each

Circle the best answer. Do not circle more than one letter. This shit's already confusing enough. Jamie's doing handstands against the wall, brainstorming ways I can come back from this. She says you should feel free to scribble in the margins if you're so inclined. You know, a stick figure me, a stick figure you, a stick figure possibility.

1. How did you feel this morning?

    A. Hungover

    B. Guilty

    C. Excited

    D. Ashamed

    E. All of the above

    F. None of the above: _____

2. Who do your kids think I am?

    A. Your friend

    B. Your personal trainer

    C. Your employee

    D. Your drinking partner

    E. All of the above

    F. None of the above: _____

3. How do you think your husband will cope with this?

    A. He will behave normally because he truly didn't see anything

    B. He will behave normally because it's easier to pretend he didn't see anything

C. He will talk himself down a rabbit hole

D. He will justify that it's not cheating if it's with a woman twenty years your junior

E. None of the above: _____

5. What is one thing you wish I understood?

A. How badly you wish you could take it back

B. How badly you wish you were single

C. The universe never has our best interests in mind

D. There is a difference between wanting and needing and most people will never know it

E. Not all decisions have consequences

F. Age gaps exist for a reason

G. None of the above: _____

6. Does our story end terribly in every possible outcome?

A. Without a doubt

B. Probably

C. Not necessarily

D. Not if we don't let it

E. This quiz is exhausting the fuck out of me

F. I need a drink

G. None of the above: _____

Essay section: 10 points each

Please answer the questions to the best of your ability. Use complete sentences only. Include a clear beginning, middle, and end. Remember, even if you can't see the end, it doesn't mean it isn't there.

1. What would you like to happen next? Please be specific. Feel free to be as unrealistic as you would like. I also have a habit of indulging.

2. Did you tell anyone about last night? Why or why not? What would you tell a confidant if you could?

3. What do you think it will be like when we see each other at the gym next? Do you think any of your friends will be able to detect the shift? Do you care if they do?

4. Do you think it's possible for two people to make each other fully happy? Why or why not?

Bonus Question: 5 points

Tell me about everyone you've ever loved before me. Make it fucking hurt.

A COMPLETE INTRODUCTION TO LITERARY HISTORY

/ Ava Hofmann

Introduction to the First Edition

[…] during the […] in the history of medieval studies […] was unearthed in a […] having acquired the property rights […] the public […] gut the […] the subterranean structure […]

[…] she […] a dead body […]

[…] held in their hands […] and […]

[…] of our perceptions of historical consciousness […] the manuscript appears […]

[…] become an object of dedicated study […] a continued campaign on the part of the […] the government to […] in underground […] lakes […] in analysis […]

[…] it has only yet been […] allow this book to see […] mixed in with the ashes […] we here at […] books […] at once […] at […] archival access […] supplant this book […]

[…] texts which serve as […] perceiving […]

[…] as a formal object embedded within a larger material system […]

[…] as ideological process […]

Archival Contexts

[…] we can reconstruct a few details of late history […]

[…] an analysis of the subterranean structure […] histories and government records […] archives which reveal […] the […] a tomb […] but supplies a name […]

[…] she was born […]

[…] not much else is known […] or her previous name […]

[…] she began to practice speaking in […] parts of her body in […]

[…] we know […] because she told us […] of life had been the subject of public executions […]

[...] testimony and court documents [...] magic [...] the arts [...]

[...] it was during this time [...]

[...] death and the [...] the burial of [...] the codex [...] this lead to an altercation [...] an in-between [...] nonconformities of [...] or witchcraft [...]

[...] a queer [...] a woman [...] whilst [...] in occult [...]

[...] an abomination [...] a burial fee [...]

[...] when a cavern of insidious intent opened up beneath their feet [...]

[...] posthumously [...] the bowels of the earth [...]

[...] one worker described the body as it [...] as if grasping at its book [...]

Archeological Analysis

[...] the conditions in which [...] for a century [...] when [...] the manuscript was [...]

[...] she [...] was bound and written [...] reoriented into landscape format [...] the original [...] has been lost [...] a print of which has been included [...]

[...] the interior of [...] is relative [...] blank space on the page verges onto [...] this [...] line-breaks [...] expensive parchment pages [...] made from sheepskin [...]

[...] can only speculate what meaning or purpose was intended to [...] to be derived from [...] labor [...]

Manuscript Analysis

[...] the primary content of the book consists [...]

[...] a collection of poems which claim to be cures or remedies [...] such collections are often known as "grimoires", or [...] "leechbooks" [...] attempts to resolve illnesses through semiotic means [...] poems [...] are often known as "charms" or "spells" [...]

[...] texts such as these tend to be [...] the difficulty of interpretation [...]

[...] the [...] the [...]

[...] the [...] reader [...] the charms can invoke [...] reading [...] as if one had found [...] literature lurking inside a [...] these

idiosyncratic formal qualities which make poems [...] and trans-
gresses [...]

[....] and in the space between [...] the charm is able to enter
[...] a kind of [...] wherein transformation occurs [...] and from
[...] the impersonal set [...] the personal springs from [...] and
even something of the subjectivity of women, despite [...]

[...] most of literature features texts [...] which [...] mutations
of [...] forms [...] the texts in the [...] the literary and symbolic
[...] of a semiotics of [...] of their [...] in so doing [...] these [...]
abstractions [...] loop back on [...] to the embodied experience of
[...] and thereby suggest [...]

[...] in other words, the poems of the [...] charms; if charms
are understood [...] an attempt to heal the body [...] an encounter
with the [...] and symbolic, and if [...] to treat the body [...] which
is written [...]

[...] she is [...] and [...]

[...] and [...]

[...] many collections of folk remedies and [...] contain [...]
contingent upon the possession of [...] contains a few particularities
which [...] pushing the text into [...] and territory [...]

[...] the invocation of the manuscript [...] as one of "common"
sentences [...] the unjust [...] powers [...] i.e., rather than [...] po-
sitions the manuscript as a work which is against power [...]

[...] text shifts between definitions of the word [...] slipping
between [...] and [...] meanings until the [...] the [...] the line, the
precise meaning of [...] is obscured [...]

[...] meanings are in some sense interchangeable [...] while
the body experiences [...] become conflated with [...] powers and
sentences [...] the human body, the body of the text, and the body
politic are [...]

[...] however, there are still several features [...] into a system
of [...] radical [...] or semiotic [...] about both the [...] readers [...]

[...] in the middle of each line [...] why do people keep speak-
ing with objects [...] double-slashes [...] the first of [...] poetic me-
ter and structure is somewhat different [...] verse forms [...] these
poems [...] guided by a prosodic technique known as [...] verse
[...] which guides line-stress [...] and structure [...] symmetries
within each line. [...] this pattern is more [...] defined [...] written
in [...] represent caesurae [...] a [...] pause [...] the middle of the

[...] verse is exactly how it sounds [...] is dictated by [...] across each line [...] lines [...]

[...] are all valid constructions [...]

[...] the answer to [...] there is a modern bias [...] to view direct address [...] to [...] and others [...] nonhuman [...] are not simply figurative [...]

[...] nature and material culture are considered [...] it is to be alive and conscious [...] with which the participation [...] can speak [...]

[...] to understand this view [...] imagine a [...] posthuman [...] a radical politics [...] we are part of a material [...]

[...] the material of lives is used in the service of radical [...] personal transformation [...]

[...] this is the beauty and the [...] power [...] and [...] of the codex [...] they are [...] she is [...] a document that [...] could never have [...]

[...] what has been dreamed of [...] an [...] archive [...] a document of [...] transformation which has [...] from the grave [...] i hope more than anything that you enjoy these texts [...]

[...] who [...] which have suffered through years of struggle [...]

[...] who [...] to arrive upon [...] your fingers, your ears, your eyes [...]

— [...]

GOOD. NOW I CAN BEGIN TO SUCK.

/ John Trefry

Exposure of the fossil corpse of a plesiosaur—in bisection with half of its remnants missing from erosion—just above the crumbling base of a steep shale escarpment—in the windscouring of the surface layer are two dorsal vertebrae, several ribs, gastralia or bellyribs, and anatomically erroneous fragments of bonefossil amidst thirtyeight gastroliths of which half are within the figuration of the corpse and half are in suspension around the corpse—, the remainder of the discovery is lying within the shale tomb, Gallery of Natural Productivity director Lawrence Mare is on an exploratory excavation with dustbrush and with a small baster puffingly blowing small quantities of inhalation from its bulb into the furrowings of bone and tabular leaves of shale, shale under the fingernails, pulverization of shale in the mustache licking his lips in daydreaming geophagy, gastroliths inside crocodiles and penguins ballastingly neutral and irrelevant to their digestion, the plesiosaur licking a chalky escarpment savouringly in a milky cloud of soluble suspension and diving to the seafloor feasting on cuttlefish lurking in the silt is accidentally ingesting several quartz and chert stones is swimming dartingly and without undue buoyancy through crosscurrents with freedom and joyous equilibrium, its corpse breaking apart in cloudy salt ink of black bile and gut chum in strong currents falling puzzlingly to the seafloor, a total of 125 gastroliths in and around the corpse,

the muscular shoulders and cirrigerous head and face of an icteric man are straining—triceps outfacing and bulging—under the fluting weight of a modillion compressing his ribs onto his diaphragm with a fabric waistband cinching beneath a buckle where the excretion of raptor feathers from a palmate orifice is halting in front of a festoon of daisies and corn and grapes covering the seam of monstrification at which his torso all over birdspikingly is below the waist becoming an ornate volutoid console rock tumbler operators in private discussion are perfecting the combination of particular kinds of silt and sulfuric acid and seeds and cinching them into a lamb abomasum inside the mechanism for the production of adequately lubricious savourstones, tabular tercets in hendecasyllabic rows in greater arrangements contingent on the inclusion of sequential fossilbed discoveries geographically across the floor of the proportionally low and expansively broad—the floor is forming a horizon—bunker enshroudingly under obscurant drapery gentleness of thin linen contouring to prows protuberances pontic depressions niches domes of incomplete sauropod skeletons from across the ADA badlands and high deserts, cartographic matrices delineating locations of gastroliths and designations of the species of monster—Seismosaurus hallorum, Cedarosaurus weiskopfae, Dinheirosaurus lourinhanensis—and coordinates of discovery and primary hunter responsible for discovery and their restingplace on stainless steel downdraft autopsy tables—exhaust fans drawing down and away dust from the skeletons themselves although the volume of the room itself is not benefitting from the same level of ventilation—only a series of boreholes through the granitic ceiling at an exploratory variety of angles—, inner office doors locking the two men in ADA jackboots with a small Rayleather snuffbox—fingertips over the abstract desertscape of its scallopingly toothy toolwork—are turning over one in the right hand of each a pair of elasmosaur savourstones from the bottom of the Baldick Sea and leaning easily on either side of the glowing embrasure clicking their teeth against the perfection of polishingly impervious granite against the tongue and palate their gloss is slicking with ionic bondage of saliva production lubriciously satisfactory, from each table a clawtag with tiny ideogram depictions—in the unmistakable hand of «the Steward»—is defining the distribution of gastroliths within the reconstruction of the skeleton including their weight and species of stone and general physiognomy—ovoid, spherical, tricylindrical, polytopic, configuration 3.4.4, configuration 4.4.4, cupolar, obround—of thousands of partial skeletons lying stately in the bunker only a meager percentage are hosting the preservation of precious digestive stones, those in possession of more than a couple of the gastroliths are in superabundant and widely varying possession, the elasmosaurus corpse deep beneath the Western Interior Seaway is bloating with the accumulation of decompositional gases in its abdomen is floating to the surface—«the ol' bloatnfloat»—with extremities forcefully at gassy attention across the surface where sharks are munching and birds landing on the adrift island of its broad back are nibbling through its sloughing skin to the cold and salty meat—analogous to the fudgy tartar of whalefish—its lower mandible is falling away from its skull sinking and its skull separating sinking separately and inconspicuously to the seafloor with the sequential deterioration of the vertebral ligaments each bone in the column is tenuously loosening in the softening offgassing sinking monster to the seafloor headless, that the stones are within the corpus of the monster is inarguable, structural branching tubular capillaries and gastric arteries in the preservation of the animal proteins collagen and actin and tubulin steeping in their own hemoglobin at the bottom of the sea or in a shallow stone depression are cagingly lacing fanvaulting above the smooth stones or in the case of skeleton KJFE 216815 within a hall of arching ribs, that the residence of the stones are foreign bodies and the product of intentional ingestion is inarguable, why the stones are lying in the corpus of the monster is extremely contentious—functioning as a gastricmill in sauropods and as ballast in plesiosaurs, or just the pleasurability of lithophagy—and a crosssection of autodidacts with daypasses to the bunker are asserting «No, the polishment of the pebbles and stones in association with the sauropod skeletons are incongruous with the lack of polishment in avian gastroliths» and «No, the abrupt rupturing of the elasmosaur cadaver and accounting for flowrates and waterdepths in the „WIS" is incongrous with the scale of the debrisfield of stones» and «No, the relative mass of stones and monster corpus—1:5346—is wildly incongruous with the relative mass of stones and avian corpus—1:11»,

«the Steward» is eating his lunch of seedy porridge and tongueprobing nettlesome seeds along his gumline is consulting the matrix and is selecting a table gingerly peeling back its linen shroud is extracting a smaller stone—dotting its outline on the mirrorplating with the felttip of his pen—that he is placing in his mouth—dry and round nearly tricylindrical with filletingly soft points ideal for postprandial sucking of this particular prandium texture—and turning over with his tongue carefully belaying its momentum toward the interior faces of his teeth but easing nudgingly along his gumline, the points of the stone are not fine enough to dig out the food between his teeth, the action is fluctuating saliva through his mouth and the oscillating friction from the intermittent matte surfaces of the stone against his gingiva is liberating the small seeds and—pressing the stone atop his tongue to the roof of his mouth—he is savouringly grinding the bonus morsels between his molars,

> the symmetry of two icteric and pogonocious men
> standing on high plinths with fixation on their ef-
> forts of stablizing their heads with their hands—
> their inboard arms are reaching over their heads
> thrusting elbows out—under the weight of two
> modillions on a cushion of strapping and twist-
> ing drapery is wending around their backs to their
> groins coquettishly belting   around behind their
> buttocks are pressing against the wall

the most compelling data against stones in the gastrickmill func-tionality hypothesis for sauropods is coming from extensive doc-umentation of experimentation on wild mataeopterae—literally «useless wing», or nominally the «great plush Ray»—the only rat-ites indigenous to ADaemone—who, analogous to all ratites, are not in possession of a crop for digestion but a cecum peristaltic with enzymes and a muscular gizzard containing a wealth of gastro-liths tumbling over themselves and processing seeds and grains in rhythmic grinding contractions continuously audible from outside the bird and visible in the quivering of fine down on its rump, re-searchers are selecting an assortment of stones—limestone, gran-ite, rose quartz—for administration to the wild Rays with necktag identification and occupying the erection of habitats of husbandly constraint, strolling in for silent slaughter with careful sorting of gizzard and proventiculus from the glop of offals and screening and washing the stones researchers are gauging duration of digestion against loss of mass and deviation in morphology from the original stones—the execution of small thumbnail delineations for compari-son—, the resultant of this perpetual grinding is however a stone of a distinctive porous matte quality with no polishment—a per-sistent argument is involving the impregnation of encoffinating salt with stomach acid creating an ideal polishing medium—, a fourth controlgroup of Rays is digesting indelible black chert pebbles, both the mass and morphological transformations of the stones as well as relative mass ratio comparisons—beast:stone and bird:stone—illustrate negligible functionality of stones in the monsters despite strikingly similar quality of stones—a light polishment is approaching that of the fossils but not quite so pristine and impervious to coagulating layers of salivary jetsam—,

analyses on the gastroliths of wild mataeopterae illustrating similar qualities to the preciously scarce savourstones of the sauropod and elasmosaur are rationalizing the explosion of countryside industrial mataeoptera farming—the fleshly byproducts of their digestive pebbles becoming ubiquitous in broths, leathercraft, liquid eggstuff, meats suitable only for grindage, and feathers for downy greatcoats—in long barracks where the majestic birds are in restraint of stocks around their thighs, the cauterization of their vicariantly vestigial wings and the clasping of long rigid tubes the length of their necks up to the background wisdom of their black eyes with connection back to a hinge that is lowering for feeding from a moldy bucket, and—with the contraversion of their instinctual dustbathing and scratching their lovers necks by braiding caduceusly together, and the pertinent stoneswallowing—their supplemental diet of rocks is via forcefeeding through a funnel with fingertips pressing over their velveteen nostrils—perpetuating and expanding under the auspices of the ADA until the seizure of a cottage industry of blackmarket artisinal rock tumblers by municipal authorities is reactivation under a more bureaucratic centralization of ADA indorgpsych—with consumption of more human laboriousness—is stripping the viability of the more durationally inefficient natural process and all mataeoptera in captivity—in excess of 215,000 in a mass extermination—except the liberation of one in the darkness by a desperate undercover veternarian whispering «Harald» watching the majestic bird limping into the sylvan selvedge—and the stockpiling of their stones in a manmade cave,

four realistically araeosystyle pairs of women in
peaceful catatonia with truncations of breastlength
plaits in long draping gathering fringingly in pleats
at their waists—with hands either across their

breasts or down at their sides or in one case around
the shoulder of her twin—are supporting shal-
low square abacuses each atop braiding annulet and
compression of bouffant echinus beneath a beam all
are burdening

«the Steward» glibly with three of his favorite savourstones click-
ing against his molars and canines turning barycentric around his
tongue discovering a small seed between his incisors is working its
apex in upward probing against the unforgiving seed tossing two
stones over the tonsillary precipice into his trachea is dying alone of
asphyxiation in the crepuscular fringes of the cavern—

PANIC FUGUE

/ Jill Khoury

he will make a purse of me
his crop and

black riding boots
search the field

for my body
but i obscure myself in

a bed of queen anne's lace
breathe small breaths

hh hh hh
hh hh hh

i give my rage
a thousand mouths

push each tongue
into the earth

PISSING CONTEST

/ Joe Sacksteder

<Messages   **Anya's Dad**   **Details**

Thurs, June 23, 8:32 PM
Remember what I told you at the door, Simon.
Whatever you do to Anya, I do to you.

8:35 PM
No worries Mr B

10:37 PM
My text better be the only buzzing
in your pocket.

10:53 PM
Simon?

10:57 PM
You don't want me texting while driving
right Mr B?

Crack your blinds and see me saying
goodnight to Anya planting nary
a demure kiss upon her cheek

10:57 PM
Good. Cutting it a little close to curfew,
are we?

Fri, July 1, 7:15 PM
What are you guys up to tonight?

7:21 PM
Pool party and bonfire at Kendalls house

No alcohol

Kendalls dads # is 801-374-0854

7:21 PM
Have fun!

7:43 PM
I'll be there in a few minutes

I know I know, whatever I do to the least
of your children you do unto me

7:43 PM
Wasn't meaning to channel the JC...
I'm going to go lift at the gym tonight.
If there's an emergency, contact Jill.

10:35 PM
Just checking in. I'm back from the gym,
icing up my shoulders.

10:47 PM
We had a great time

I'll have Anya home before curfew
with her hymen intact

10:47 PM
Everything better be intact, jokester.

Wed, July 6, 6:42 PM
Public skate, huh?

7:01 PM
Yeah

11:13 PM
Anya really likes you. I can tell.

11:53 PM
Things are going well

11:53 PM
I think she's just a little unsure if you feel
how she feels.

Thurs, July 7, 12:01 AM
I'm unsure why she'd feel that way

12:01 AM
So you're both unsure. Maybe if you
were more openly affectionate…

12:03 AM
Should we be talking about this?

12:03 AM
Kids go to public skate. It's almost a
little toooo wholesome.

12:08 AM
I've been trying to avoid reciprocation
by her weight-lifting dad duh

12:08 AM
Come on, Simon, I'm not that bad
looking of a guy.

12:12 AM
Hahahahahah

Fri, July 8, 8:38 PM
Anya came home in tears

8:44 PM
?!?

I brought her home

She wasn't in tears...

8:45 PM
She's in tears now.

8:49 PM
I'll call her

8:49 PM
I don't think she wants to talk to you
tonight.

9:00 PM
But we had a really fun night

We went for a walk at the arboretum

Then to that new fondue restaurant

9:00 PM
I think she just can't help but be a little
disappointed. Like you can't bear the idea
of touching her.

9:09 PM
I don't get it

Are you saying you'll ease off
some of the overprotectiveness

9:10 PM
I'm saying relationships evolve. If you weren't
eighteen years old, you'd know that.

9:17 PM
You're eighteen, right?

9:17 PM
Barely

Sat, July 9, 12:02 PM
Care to explain yourself?

12:03 PM
Oh no

Is she upset again

12:03 PM
No, she seems radiantly happy.
Do you know anything about this?

12:04 PM
Maybe

We went to brunch

12:04 PM
Is that all...?

12:07 PM
We made out. You said relationships
evolve and you'd ease up on being
so overprotective...

12:07 PM
So you thought that meant you could
just do whatever? Is it overprotective
not to want my daughter's purity dragged
through the mud?

12:10 PM
This is getting weird

I think I might need to take some
time away from your whole

family no offense

11:09 PM
Simon, are you awake?

Jill's still away at her bowling night. I wanted
to take this time to apologize for how
I've been behaving. To be honest, the first
time I said that thing to you about how
whatever you did to Anya, etc., the words
felt so awkward. That's why I repeated it in
a text. I thought that maybe I could make it
sound tough but a little playful like the
comedian I heard on Conan.

But I kept thinking about it too much.

I want you to know that none of this is
Anya's fault. I'm okay that you guys made
out--happy even--and I'll try not to
interfere as much in the future.

I guess you're asleep.

Or angry.

Sun, July 10, 11:32 AM
Sorry neither

I left my phone in the car and
slept late

I didn't talk to Anya yesterday or
make any rash decisions

Glad to hear.

11:32 AM
So no harm done

11:37 AM
Do you guys have upcoming plans?

Thurs, July 14, 4:57 PM
Great seeing you at the gym! How long
have you been going there?

6:03 PM
Just started

6:09 PM
Well, let me know if you need a spotter.

Do you guys have upcoming plans?

7:14 PM
Hahahahah my arms would snap in half
if I tried to reciprocate spotting

We're going to a movie

7:14 PM
What're you seeing?

7:48 PM
No worries. Be safe.

Sat, July 16, 9:08 AM
Simon. I'm really sorry to hear about you
and Anya. She told me. I thought you
guys really might have a future together.

12:10 PM
Yeah bummer

I really like Anya but she said we were
stagnant and I wasn't exciting enough

12:10 PM
Well, on the one hand, it's nice to be
unfettered so you can pursue other
exciting things. But, if you really like her,
you could try to win her back. Something
tells me her feelings aren't dead.
Whatever it takes.

2:36 PM
Thanks Mr B

2:37 PM
At the very least, see you by the dumbbells.
You're really making progress!

Sure thing

4:39 PM
WHAT DID YOU DO TO ANYA?!?

4:42 PM
What's wrong?

She happy again?

4:42 PM
She's "never felt so liberated."

4:50 PM
You know what I don't care

I'll tell you

She tied me up + gagged me +
whipped me with one of my school
ties

That was what really freaked me out
initially

That's the kind of stuff she likes

4:50 PM
Is that all?

She pissed on my chest

And wouldn't let me cum

How DARE you talk about my daughter
like that?

She's the one who wanted to do it!

I was the one who was scared

You remember what I said I'd do?

Are you following that thought through
to its conclusion?

I'm pretty sure that would mean
you're getting pissed on

I will fuck you up.

I get it

A promise is a promise right?

*

Do you want your daughter's boyfriend to tie you up and piss on
your chest? No. Not even a little? No. Not even to see how power-
ful his stream is, to see if he's cut or not? No. Is your daughter's
boyfriend ugly? Yes. Try having another daughter. No. And you truly

don't want him to piss on you? No. You're lucky. Live out the rest of your days tormented by petty challenges.

*

SURFRAJET® 30-SECOND MEDIA SPOT

INT. GYM — DAY

MR. BOWDEN (50) on the leg press machine at the gym. He is wearing one of those sleeve-less shirts cut underneath each arm, expos-ing his TONED RIBS.

The plates rising and falling in time with UPBEAT INDIE ROCK.

Mr. Bowden GRIMACING and SWEATING with exer-tion.

                    VOICE (V.O.)
          Some promises are meant to last a
          lifetime.

SIMON (18) taps Mr. Bowden on the shoulders after he's done with his set. Mr. Bowden looks back up at Simon, his smile tinged with embarrassment. Simon is simultaneous-ly slight of frame and a little doughy, his arms insignificant. He GESTURES COQUETTISHLY towards the machine as if to ask if it's available.

                    VOICE (V.O.) (cont'd)
          But even though our desires re-
          main true, sometimes our bodies
          betray us.

Mr. Bowden reaches for a towel and spray

bottle to clean off the machine. Simon waves
him away with a laugh.

Mr. Bowden puts his arm around Simon and
turns to face the camera.

> MR. BOWDEN
> When I entered into a triangular
> relationship with my daughter and
> her boyfriend--

> SIMON
> (interrupting)
> Husband.

> MR. BOWDEN
> I thought I could foresee the
> mess of complications sure to
> face us. What I couldn't foresee
> was erectile dysfunction.

> SIMON
> Surfrajet helps men with erectile
> dysfunction get and keep an erec-
> tion.
> (winking)
> As do I.

INT. SAUNA — DAY

Mr. Bowden and Simon enter a sauna. With a
spoon, Simon splashes Mr. Bowden with water
from the wooden bucket. The other MEN IN THE
SAUNA look at one another and SMILE KNOW-
INGLY.

> MR. BOWDEN
> (at camera)
> Surfrajet, it's not just for

men who never loved their aging
wives.

                    SIMON
        Though it'll work for that too.

                         EVERYONE
            I guess…

Everyone LAUGHS.

                                   FADE OUT.

                        *

                        Yes. No big deal. It's an or-
dinary pain. Does your daughter's boyfriend want to piss on your
chest? No. Decide what's worse, an eternity of void or living with
a rat sewn in your stomach. Yes. Congratulations! Is he pissing on
your chest right now? Yes. Have your eyes just followed this flow to
get you hard? Yes. Whatever it takes, man. No. Close your fucking
laptop and live in the moment. No. Are you worried you're just be-
ing tricked? Yes. Does the boyfriend hold some kind of longstanding
grudge that he might be avenging through abject humiliation and/
or blackmail?

                        *

        SCOTT FREE AND CLEAR® LAUNDRY DETERGENT
                30-SECOND MEDIA SPOT

INT. SUNLIGHT-DRENCHED UPSCALE MUDROOM — DAY

BLURRY LENS coming into focus, MONTAGE
SHOTS of SIMON (18), playing with his TWO
SONS (2, 5). The wash has just finished, and
clean clothes spill from laundry baskets
like fruit from a cornucopia. The humans are
freshly showered, glowing.

Simon's long hair is pulled back with a HEADBAND, cut sharply below the ears. Occasionally a strand of hair falls forward across his face and he has to SHAKE IT BACK. You wouldn't think the haircut would look good on a guy, but you'd be surprised.

> SIMON (V.O.)
> Due to the byzantine rules of a unique gentleman's agreement, when my wife gave birth to two sons, Prescott and Roo, her father was forced to adopt and financially support two sons on the side with me.

MR BOWDEN (64) enters the room, looking tired but happy. His hair is losing ground on two battlefronts, color and thickness.

> MR. BOWDEN
> (to camera)
> When Tiberius was born, we definitely noticed some skin irritation, some baby acne.

Shot of TIBERIUS to show that the condition has been fixed by laundry detergent so the viewers won't worry.

> MR. BOWDEN (cont'd)
> We knew that, like my daughter and Simon, Simon and I needed to switch to a really great detergent.

> SIMON
> (to camera)

```
So we switched, my wife and I
and her father and I, to Scott
Free And Clear. And I don't think
we'll ever switch back.

                MR. BOWDEN
(picking up the kid who isn't Tiberius)
Not only is it gentle, but it
works on really tough stains: red
wine, ink, grease, jazz, grass
stains, blood, patriarchy--

                  SIMON
              (interrupting)
Urine.

                MR. BOWDEN
                 (smiling)
Take it from the experts. Scott
Free And Clear, for whatever
taints your day.

                        FADE TO BLACK.


                    *
```

No. Have you Googled his name, ransacked the digital archives of his life? Have you scrolled him younger and younger via his Instagram posts to ascertain the full magnitude of your sickness? No. Best just to get drunk and turn off all inhibitions, clicking erratically, and hope that he doesn't have an app or whatever that lets him track who's been curious all over his profiles. (Of course, if he does, it could force the issue to the surface.) Yes. Is your doubt perhaps a symptom, along with myriad feelings of worthlessness, brought on by years of not admitting, even in liminal soliloquys, that you indeed want your daughter's boyfriend to tie you up + gag you + piss on your chest?

*

AFTERLIFE INSURANCE® 30-SECOND MEDIA SPOT

INT. ICE RINK — DAY

A family of eleven is at an ice rink, ice
skating. MR. BOWDEN (78) is proud of his
clan but looks a little winded. His daughter
ANYA (18) and son-in-law SIMON (we're talk-
ing barely 18 here) are holding hands. The
eight total children they're collectively
raising are playing predator/prey or some
other murder-based game of Darwinian sur-
vival: PRESCOTT (18), ROO (18), LOKI (18),
TIBERIUS (18), SAM JR. (18), SIMON JR. (18),
ODIN (18), and TRIFF (18).

             VOICE (V.O.)
    When you're gone, who will look
    after them?

Mr. Bowden skates up next to Simon, and
Simon reluctantly drops Anya's hand. Mr.
Bowden is bald, and all of his once impres-
sive muscles have gone limp like melting wax
or deflating balloons or whatever.

Everything has gone right for Simon always.
The world is a joke, and he knows the punch
line, the shaggy dog that's being withheld
from the rest of us until it's too late to
laugh without getting put in a home.

             MR. BOWDEN
            (unheard)
    I didn't realize what the stat-
    ute of limitations was on our ar-
    rangement. We don't need to keep

Anya involved.

                    VOICE (V.O.)
You can't heat your home with
memories.

                    SIMON
               (surprised, unheard)
Mr. B, I love Anya. I love our
four sons. I love what we've got.

                    VOICE (V.O.)
Who will do to your son-in-law
whatever he does to your daughter
when you're no longer around to
dispense threats?

One of the kids SLIPS and FALLS, and Anya
helps him up. Everyone is smiling. It's a
lovely day.

                    MR. BOWDEN
                  (unheard)
How's that possible? After you've
gone behind her back for years?

                    SIMON
                  (unheard)
I had to go behind her back if I
wanted you to go behind hers. At
first when you threatened me at
your doorstep, I figured you just
wanted to fuck your daughter like
a normal man. I never knew things
would go so far.

                    VOICE (V.O.)
We're on this earth for such a
short time.

MOMENTS LATER
Mr. Bowden is on his back, clutching his
chest. The camera looks down on him, rotat-
ing, the screen slowly bleaching out.

Simon kneels down beside Mr. Bowden.

                    MR. BOWDEN
              (struggling to be unheard)
          I'll never stop threatening to
          fuck you. I only wish that my de-
          sires--
                    (last gasp)
          had been even less thinly veiled.

                    SIMON
                    (laughing)
          Hahahahahah!

                                   FADE TO WHITE.

                         *

          Is your daughter's boyfriend eighteen? No. I
mean, wait until he is, okay? Yes. Do you actually care about your
daughter's feelings? Yes. Hahahahahah proceed to No. No. Is all you
need courage? No. Is it even more complicated than it seems? Yes.
No big deal. It's an ordinary pain. No. Are you telling me that all
you need is run-of-the-mill courage? Yes. People have gone to war.

RIVER ON FIRE

/ Daniel Bailey

The world usually does not learn your name
and when it does, it's not
for good reasons, which is why
I'm at my lowest when I feel
like I know who I am

When my habits and desires meet
on a burnt out road:
the automatic thought beginning
I feel...
\

\
\

I stream video of burning rivers
smell my body in search of the same chemicals
that let the river catch fire

Toddling through spiderwebs
I become attached to the world
Its reasons for being endure me long
enough for me to endure myself

A prayer against life is a prayer
in which I am paved into the road
skulled in place where forest was shaved
into something useful: a dumpster island
behind a place of 24 hour commerce
and now they really know who I am
and now I really know me as me
now I can endure as a brick: a shadow
of a mountain developed in bursts

ENDURE THE CALM

/ Daniel Bailey

In the hours before the storm
I imagine the wind through the trees
as a round of applause by the leaves for the leaves
and how the trees stretch and warm up
for the storm now miles behind the wind
I breathe out of my cocoon
flow the rapids of my blood
try to notice whatever mineral structure
has formed in my veins
flow around the tiny obstructions
that may one day stroke me away
to light up my pulse with brine
prepare the fluorescent tomb
that I'll pass through like sediment
or like plankton trapped in the gills
crack shadows like eggs whose yolk
ignites upon the objects of light's obstruction
crack plastic succulents and drink the crude oil
become the storm before the storm preceding storm

SKIP INTRO

/ Jodi Bosin

i wish i had three hearts, like a squid
i feel for the ribs under my skin

deep breaths, seven seconds in,
get through this minute, and then the next

lean my head back and the wall's right there,
dependable, i just need a second

a mini snickers is like a tiny present
the holiday ones are shiny red

there's a mini snickers for every occasion
perfect squares made by robot hands

carly is crocheting unicorn horns for her nieces
on the other couch

and alex has fallen asleep,
familiar scene, peaceful and easy

we stay up all night watching LOST
white text warping around on a black screen

i know that when i go to sleep i'll dream
of you, like i always do, i'll dream we're together

and wake up alone and disoriented
the same stupid thing every single night

jesus fucking christ, it's exhausting
circles of hell circling like vultures

opening text fading into the stars
with the tyranny of longing

HIPPOCRATES

/ Jodi Bosin

Lately I feel nauseous and every few hours a panic wells up inside me like bile. I'm distracted. Everyone has an opinion but nobody actually knows anything. Especially me. Even just seeing your name in a text makes me ACHE! Lose whatever progress I thought I had made, etc. The power one person can have, and all of it circumstance. I could just as easily have met someone else, but I met you, and the space you left is shaped like you and now no one else can fit there. My thoughts take the shape of your face, the first thing I saw on so many mornings, soft from sleep and beautiful, looking at me. My empty hands, your knuckles, knobby in that particular way, okay, you get the idea. I unfollowed you on everything so I don't see you but I still feel you. I feel everything, under my skin, digested, making me sick. What is on the other side of this, flip the flat earth over, guts. It's easiest at home when everyone's around, tungsten light of the lamps, someone laughing and miller high life, a record playing. Dim sum and sun lighting our hair, in a booth by the window, I would die without friends, or maybe I'm already dead. Fear-of-future feeling, all-consuming. Surrounded by everyone else's relationships. The whole day passed and I didn't even see it. I was looking for you, but you're not there.

OUT OF BODY

/ Jodi Bosin

There is a feeling of being disconnected. The only way I can think to describe it is a hyper awareness of being two eyes looking out of a head. I try to describe it in a different way but just think that same thought over and over again. Like being in a dream, everything slightly curved like a fish-eye lens or a peephole in a front door or the edge of the world. That far away feeling when you're talking to someone and you look at them for too long and they begin to recede, and you're dizzy, do you know what I mean. Something like that. The sensation is scary, it feels like mortality, it feels like loss of control, like being alone, like all the worst things. The psychiatrist called this "depersonalization" and said it is normal. Maybe you're just more aware of it now, she said. What does that mean... I look down at my hands and they seem far away and unattached to me. Or it's that I feel too often, too acutely, the limits of being human, lately. But it was you who detached, from me. Where are you going?

EA SPORTS LIVE LULLABY

/ Jodi Bosin

the feeling of something misplaced / looking for a thing you
know is lost / it was right here / i put it right here / where
could it have gone / i'm different than i was before / i don't
say sorry anymore / i say what i mean and i don't take it back /
i exfoliate once a week / and when someone offers to do some-
thing for me i say okay, thanks / i'm reading on the couch and
behind me i hear alex cooking and eating crackers / i do push-
ups every day / i like the ambient sounds of my roommates / i
burned sage to rid the house of you / it didn't work, obviously /
you're too deep and i'm trying to keep / there are three to five
coffee mugs around the living room at any given time / this used
to annoy me but now it's fine / actually i like it, it reminds me
that i'm not alone / nothing bothers me like it used to / after
the worst thing happens and i'm still here / you know? / my
skin isn't thin anymore / i'm friends with my co-workers / we
get dinner and they make me laugh / i make patches with positive
phrases / and write affirmations on a piece of paper i keep in my
wallet / where your "i love you" note used to be / i got the wal-
let the day we broke up actually / i never had a chance to show
you / there was a lot i never got to say / alex is playing the soc-
cer video game, the one with the british announcers / it's dark
at 5pm now and what happened to all our plans / from the third
floor i hear them playing, faintly, when i fall asleep / he's one on
one with the goalkeeper / the noise is comforting / anchored to
something / lullaby

Unity of opposites

from Wikipedia, the free encyclopedia

/ **Jodi Bosin**

The unity of opposites is the central category of <u>dialectics</u>, said to be related to the notion of <u>non-duality</u> in a deep sense.[1] It defines a situation in which the existence or identity of a thing (or situation) depends on the co-existence of at least two conditions which are opposite to each other, yet dependent on each other and presupposing each other, within a field of tension.

(1)

We sat on the end of the bar on Monday and you kept running your fingers along the corner, picking at a triangle shaped spot where the wood had come off. Hands right there and so familiar but so far away. This is an exercise in falling. The way I miss you is white hot and burning, heart in a clenched hand, all day, tense, I am miserable and electric with the feeling of it.

Lately I am restless and aware of everything, the way Spider-Man sees and how things slow down in a car crash in a movie. I am angry at you for doing this to me, for telling me you're sad and keeping busy, I don't feel sorry, I feel fury. I guess this is why people say we shouldn't Be Friends. But on the other hand, fuck what everyone else says (except the tarot card reader who told me to follow my intuition). I can't follow every thought to its conclusion, now, when nothing makes sense. I just feel and/or fall instead. Here I am, live and in person and in pain.

This morning was a long, long time ago.

(2)

On Saturday the comic book store slash café played Christmas music, many times, many ways. You're wearing that big grey sweater I loved to borrow, how it swallowed me up and how it smelled like you. Stages of hell I didn't know existed, imagining never touching you again, chief among them. I'm out of explanations. When did Christmas become another Valentine's day and the world revolve around romance, spitting it in my face?

There's a tree in the corner and signs about "Small Business Saturday Sale" on yellow paper taped up everywhere. The small round tables are comic themed, it's cute, ours is the Captain America shield. I notice a piece of hair behind your ear that's longer than the rest. The worst thing is the not-knowing, the no-choice of it. My lows are deep and my highs are a manic sense of calm slash hope. I feel everything everywhere and all at once. Furious and desperate, to be your friend and to never see you again. War of opposites.

The universe expands and I am more alive than ever.

Qs AND As

/ Susan Falco

Short is hard but powerful.

     —Ander Monson, "The Essay Is the Egg"

A: I tried to fit "I hope you are lucky enough not to have to burn your books for fire or food" on to an embroidered pillow, but it was too long. Embroidery requires selectivity, just as selecting which books to burn in the night. Which to keep: your toes or your Tolstoy?

A: You tell me that an image can be a story, that a postcard is no less than a letter. You say that the process of writing that story MATTERS to someone. You say that time does not have to move in a line. That fractured can be whole.

    Q: I don't know how anyone alive outlines and writes a memoir. How do you structure a story when you don't know how it ends? How can anyone shape a memoir when they cannot step back far enough to see the shape of their own life?

    A: The goal is to see the forest AND the trees. Even in the truth, especially in the truth, the reader is looking for a conflict-crisis-resolution. Don't you want to see something change?

Q: How does the writer tell the truth when the truth is nothing changes?

A: If the writer perceives no change, then that writer isn't looking hard enough. Either that, or the story isn't true. Because everyone knows that change is the only constant and entropy the only law.

A: Addiction is repetition and blindness, writing is change and perspective.

Q: Can writing a picture of a thing change the nature of the thing? Can a lie change the truth? What is my way in to the story when the story is unbearable to tell?

A: I am trusting the voice behind my voice. I am trying to trust the voice behind my voice. I am trying to see myself with compassion. I am exploring my dreams.

I was speeding away from myself in the back of a pickup truck.

Michael, high on Xanax, giggling idiotically, kept grabbing me, throwing me in the back of the truck playfully, like it was a joke. I fought and yelled "I'm fucking serious," but he lifted me over the tailgate.

Then my shadow twin came. I fought her with a stick. Michael dropped me and started to drive. "Go, go," I shouted. "I don't like what she's doing with that stick."

A: Robert Johnson took three days to die. His whiskey poisoned by a jealous man, it ate through him bit by bit. And all this because of a woman! And she doesn't even matter to the story. He told the world he was the devil's own, sprinkled powders at the doorway, the same powders his grandmother would have used to ward off dogs. Something in the herbs makes dogs temporarily nose-blind, so a pack of hell hounds can't sniff out, say, a child on his way north hiding under the floorboards. So it still wards off evil in 1933, this powder.

A: The Powder of the Angels and I'm Yours. —Jayne Anne Phillips

Q: The powder of the angels and I'm yours?

A: I think he quit protecting his doors, his windows.

I think he invited the devil in, and the devil ate him.

I think he was ready to leave, but good God what a brutal way to go.

Q: Does being ill give you insight in to love? Into madness? Is that why John Keats is so different than the rest, because he's sick? How can physical feelings exist on the page, how do I write fever and bone-ache? Do I want to? Am I selfish to want to write bone hurt? To want to say things that will make other people feel bad, that will probably ensure that my FAVORITE people will feel at least a tiny bit bad when they read it. My wish is to put together, not to take apart.

A: Time is already the greatest of deconstructionists.

Q: How do I protect my doors, my windows?
   How do I recite a spell to keep the devil out?
   I am not ready to leave. When I go let me go gently.

How can hybridity recreate a fractured memory in a way other genres cannot? Because it's messy? Because it's kind?

A: My Patron Goddess of Hybridity is the Sphinx, who, (as the former owner of my copy of *Family Resemblance* wrote in the margins "eats you if you fuck up.")

Q: I have been asking myself where I go when I leave. Who is the shadow woman, who operates my body when I am gone? When my eyes are black holes?

A: The Blackout happens in the sunken place, beneath the waves. Deep in the trench where pale monsters oscillate in the ocean current, Blackout blooms. There is horror in this place but there is power, too.

Q: How do I use language to access that deep subconscious collective unconscious Deep Deep Down The Deep and Wet One The Maenad The Siren The Lamia The Terrible Beauty. How do I use language to talk about repression, duality, divided identity, fluid identity, doppelgängers and Shadow-Things? How do I use language as a performance?

A: Jayne Anne Phillips's *Black Tickets* showed me how to use language to grab someone hard. Her short sharp fever dreams made me feel like cracked glass, they are sharp as diamonds. They gleam but I wouldn't want to live in one.

Q: Aren't you living in the story you are writing? Where else could you be? What would it be like to want to tell stories? To tell stories someone might *want* to hear instead of (maybe?) *need* to hear? Although, the last thing anyone else wants to hear are other people's dreams. What about visions?

Q: What if I want to interact with the images, characters, and places that intrigue me in a place where there are no rules, where I can manipulate the fabric of space and time like a Goddess? What if I want to lucid dream on the page? Where does control matter in to the creative process, and how do I keep the dream controlled but still a dream, at what points do I shut out the wild magic?

A: I want to control the dream.

I want not to go flying in to space.

I'm afraid of flying off in to space: the loss of control, the whooshing upwards.

A: My Writer Self, or "Sport Jacket Susan": Part lizard/Part Fairy Queen.

My Black Dress Self: Drella (Half Cinderella Half Dracula.)

My Catholic Self: Pearls and Regrets

My Remembered Self: Unforgivable

Q: I'd like to take the reader by the hand, to reach through the page and connect, but I don't want to scare anyone. Because memory is not an orderly, chronological filing cabinet, writing about the past need not be an evidence file. How can I connect gently?

A: A Victorian lass sits at her embroidery sampler. She drips belladonna in her eyes and rouges her cheeks to recreate the dilation and flush of fever. She embroiders a milk maid with red shoes. She cannot imagine her future, so she leans in over her creation.

A: A young girl in China in 1933 embroiders her tiny shoes, shoes which her feet are being re-shaped to fit. She eats red bean dumplings to soften the bones of her feet, to prepare herself for molding, to grow in to a new shape. The shoes are to show her husband's family what she envisions for her future. Frogs to prevent the wet season maladies. Coins for luck and money. Mirrors to ward off hungry ghosts. She is sewing shoes to last a life time. She traces her husband's foot on to the cloth to cut the pattern, she repeats the pattern until her fingers are stiff. She sews them together three at a time, then stitches the layers together until it forms a sole. Her stitches always mean something. She can control this shoe, and so she tries to shape it to fit her future.

A: I choose my words for brevity and power. I have chosen my words because of the larger things they hint at. I can control the page and so I shape it to fit my future. I've always had an unhealthy relationship with the future: I have not been expecting it. I didn't care for anything because I was not asking anything to last.

Q: So what happens now?

FROM **WYRD] BIRD**

/ Claire Marie Stancek

Again, blood.

New snow clings to dead trees

and living trees

dead in winter. The silos and the barns and the fields. The grey sky the grey fields. A strange power enters me in sleep. In a vision you are holding your dick, which is fat and soft like a lung. Within the rhythm of the sentence remain the rhythm of our breath still, now and always. To roam backwards on the train track, to reach back into time.

The etymology of the word conversation is "to turn around together."

Let us be, as Milton, *Smit with the love of sacred song.*

Let us have forever, suspended with Eve in grammatical possibility.

> *But wherefore all night long shine these, for whom*
> *This glorious sight, when sleep hath shut all eyes?*

The word worms through the bloodthick wound flesh of my human brain.

An illuminated grid falls aslant into this world from another one. World, what : the sky? With silence, you /filled me. Or/ with you I am filled with silence.

Wreathes around lampposts, my breath interwreaths in air with my walkers, my momentary companions in a haze and then you find you never knew each other

anymore, like how easy it would be

to fall apart in this falling apart. The stupid things we wanted like, to live a good life. The man on the street is falling apart and everyone pretends not to see.

Exhaust exhalations.

The concept of divine Providence suggests that from evil, God will always bring forth good. I cannot find—among the ill spring that brings forth buds into time gone wrong, among plastic dumps, and ongoing war, among institutionalized racism and refugees arrested or turned away—part or even haphazard recompense. Whatever beauty populates a day seems sinister against the world the withering world. Like how my glass casts a pattern—diamond shapes among shadow, lined each with a barely perceptible rainbow. Or how I heard your voice in a dream, as clear as though you spoke to me in life. Or how the smell of some neighbor cooking returns to me a memory from infancy: stumbling beside you barefoot, along a pebble path. It is not enough, O God, to ward off death, and to God I say, it is not enough

to ward off the spread of death.

But Milton was already following these labyrinths, when in the voice of his Satan he fashioned two rhetorical snail shells and set them opposite one another on pentameter's smooth tessellated surface:

> *If then his Providence*
> *Out of our evil seek to bring forth good,*
> *Our labour must be to pervert that end,*
> *And out of good still to find means of evil.*

And later, *Evil be thou my Good.*

This second more compressed version draws the two wound shells close into one wound interwound, so that Good and Evil each breathe the other's breath, impossible to tell whose exhalation condenses damp on whose hot cheek.

You said the word *reverie* and a sound of wings charged the air.
What shining in window's glare-brimming glass.

And I saw the sunlight drench the people around us in a dreamy
haze, turn the graffiti on the brick walls into shining half-formed
prophecies, and elevate us both in mutual wonder.

The train rushes over the highway by means of a magical bridge. I
was given a word in my dream, but how do I define this word, and
when should I use it, and to whom. Empty time

all the time.

The wand in the trees.

Shadows & light flashing running down the length of the train. I
looked at my mother looking into every window

Couldn't catch her eye. A superstition grows on me like moss.
Lichen liken, like: animacy of the world. I believe the woods spoke
silence sentient. Empty me as we empty. Away goes where you go.

If our bodies sit side by side on the train, our spirits roam else-
where. Other-where.

Babbling air.

Empty] Unearthing
wand] way blunt stubs beckoned, like hands, rapaciously
babbling] ablative

/ side b

2016.31

/ Bradley J. Fest

How many more people can make a career out of denouncing some part of the present as neoliberal?
   "I mean I certainly will."

   —#GagaintheThroneRoom, *The Eschatology Index*

Come on. Chin up. The irony enterprise has many more bold missions ahead.[1]
(It's in the contract.) Sure, portions of the dusty porch of middle age cast wide
shadows over time's timid canopy. "I mean, people below play *Pokémon Go*,
and the gears keep grinding. '*I caught a cute armored rhinoceros.*'" Our sad

maverick past stalks us. We *never* learn.[2] The days clip by, unstilled,
unmeasured. But it is also not 1982. Or 1946. We are not quite millenarians.[3]
Nor caduceus-waving hollows. We neither read nor write enough,
and our institutions are scorched and wailing,[4] oozing their last few pustules

into the anarchic temporal stream below our dangling and fetid limbs.[5]
It must change. No one has any other answer. "'At least, that any of us
can see.'"[6] Must we ever suffer these speculative parallactic doomtopias,
crushing our imaginations with their cuddly panoptic pet-rock-as-

intellectual-property. Sigh. Redundancy. Where else to go, what else to do,
how else to move in and out of these moments, these disastrous
   fleeting moments.

Epigraph in the spirit of #GagaintheThroneRoom, *The Eschatology Index: Trump Vogue*, vol.
3 (Pittsburgh, PA: TSFHSB, 2027). The AI-takeover of the series has been widely de-
manded by the fans, and the result is generally agreed to be quite good. I have found the
DJ-algorithm for the apocalypse rave. Next up, auditioning an astounding opening act.
1   One would hope.
2   See Jonathan Schell, *The Fate of the Earth* (New York: Farrar, Straus and Giroux, 1982).
3   See Norman Cohn, *The Pursuit of the Millennium: Revolutionary Millenarians and Mystical Anarchists
of the Middle Ages*, rev. and exp. ed. (1957; repr., New York: Oxford University Press, 1970).
4   In other words: *come on*, this one is not so bad either. See Bradley J. Fest, "2013.03," *Spork*, June
30, 2013, http://archive.sporkpress.com/2013/06/30/3-poems-brad-fest-pt-12/.
5   Like hyperspace in Iain M. Banks, *Consider Phlebas* (1987; repr., New York: Orbit, 2008).
6   But really, is this not always already the case? Is not our problem, precisely, the opposite? Too

2016.33

/ Bradley J. Fest

Not democracy yet. Not tomorrow, but at least a couple of months
away, is…This year is still not over. Goddamn.[8] 2016 lacks any
sense of an ending.[9] "Rather, the elites are swarming my humiliated feet,
eating self-reliance hacktivist tracts that they hope are nourishing,

at least sometimes. The annual rhythms, the sense of possibility
and autumnal decay ('no matter the necropolitics of an exhausted
culture')—we tramp these burdened paths together, sinking into dismal
campus novels. All these new possible collectives, gasping and dying in

the instants of first meeting: should the new dancing occur across
the somatic fugues of past grammar lessons deadening our new
pedagogic summer shimmer of like right now? Well, we have
stamina, absorbing, waxing, overcoming our love of the mirror,

the lamp, the rest." But tomorrow and then…Wasteland cold
blowing out of the future nonetheless; what tired fantasies, what hope.

---

much change!? See Rosa Lyster, "The Best Time I Pretended I Hadn't Heard of Slavoj Žižek,"
Hairpin, July 14, 2016, https://thehairpin.com/the-best-time-i-pretended-i-hadnt-heard-of-
slavoj-%C5%BEi%C5%BEek-4d746d77606#.yp3l0dhrt. Bang bang.

7   Or… see Fredric Jameson, An American Utopia: Dual Power and the Universal Army, ed.
Slavoj Žižek (New York: Verso, 2016), https://www.youtube.com/watch?v=MNVKoX40ZAo.

8   I keep thinking I can just write the last poem in the series, but the boundedness of this cer-
tain limit creases my laboring mind.

9   It is really screwing up a lot of plans; so, in the words of a generic mid-1990s East Coast
hardcore band, "Let. The. Lines. Extend!"

2016.36: PREFACE

/ Bradley J. Fest

And then all the voices… at once decohered and fused, were flattened
and set adrift, emulsified, sounding their horrific horizonless eternity-squall
with inscrutable cacuminal psycho-acousmatic resonance,[10] different registers
ringing oppressively monotonic, lines singled up,[11] individuality squelched

in the black hole of 2016, like matter's end, a game in extra-innings slowly abandoned,
crushed by the weight of all this absurd historiography, this creeping fascism,[12]
numerals designating some *new* thing (and not just the same old failures)…
they all just sort of *stopped*, quit speaking. Some, after a time, ventured explanations:

vibrant matter; economic fundamentalism; postnatural anthrocide; Clinton;
"cultural anxiety."[13] "We" attempted, for brief moments of inhalation (a month
here, there), to quantify and measure everything ourselves to (best) fit the persistent
regime(s), the ridiculous logic of this melancholic era, these dismal years ahead,

their silencing, their univocity, their inhuman rationale, the despair. In the horrific
light of the present, can anyone still convince themselves that it was ever *really*
about the dancing?[14] The rock and roll killing machine?[15] Sure, in audacious youth,
but today? Perhaps someday it will be *only* the dance or else *something important*

about harmony. But now there is climate change and the constant hateful crimes
of the United States and its illiterate avatar and a silence. No matter how much
we inject alternatives into time's inarticulate penumbral refusal—our longest hair
swirling around our jaundiced eyes and slow regrets and ecstatic reflections

---

10   See Michel Chion, *The Voice in Cinema* (1982), trans. Claudia Gorbman (New York: Columbia
University Press, 1999).

11   See Thomas Pynchon, *The Crying of Lot 49* (1966; repr., New York: Harper Perennial Modern
Classics, 2006), 20, and *Against the Day* (New York: Penguin, 2006), 3.

12   Early yesterday morning Donald J. Trump was elected President of the United States of Amer-
ica.

13   Et cetera, et et et cetera.

14   So this is, by all accounts, where this "sonnet" should conclude, and that should be it. Project
and collection complete. Send it out. But. #2017 is a new dispensation.

in this annual February sadness window—we still just have atmospheric song
mixing our nostalgic hardcore pasts: what shame and recrudescent hairdos,
what sonic cataracts obscure our philosophic grunts. Exalt the last distorted guitar
wailing like the worst 1990s cliché into its own irrelevant turbometal future;

without the requisite symphonic death growls, it means nothing. I suppose
in what follows I had desired to construct some alternative communications
network by multiplying the speakers attempting to navigate the chilling aisles
of modern temporality, perhaps; but with who, with boom moon you, with nope?

Gone. Clairvoyance, disambiguation, coldness, writing, repeal,[16] hypermultivocity,
bang. There will be at least four speakers.[17] And then a backsliding into
equipacious opera, *luftig* satiety in the circuits of drive, all us digital beings
streamed into the weird dispensations offered by a YouTube life, by the pitiful

pantheistic market-driven escapism we'd all bought overwhelming
stock options in, divesting our better natures, stuttering sick syncopations into
an even poorer understanding of the flashes from overdetermined historical time—
real screaming. While we shred on mandolins in the mathrock justly conferred

on our belated long hair, planetarity accepts crisis; deeply abiding our failures
it goes along, helpless and headless. I want better prose futures. I tell people
about them. They listen. And then… nothing. No word, no rejection, no dismissal.
Just… taciturnity. It was all those sundry devils who'd sometimes deign to tear

at my ocular implants years ago[18]: search committees can sense that kind of corruption.
It oozes out of the scattered fines littered across my mottled dark angioplasty
and carcinogenic complexion. Wiggle. So there will be a couple sonnets
about escaping the planet. Here, now, stranded in a 2017 beyond the bounds

of the form's artificially imposed structural limitations, during this cruelest
month in academe, there is only a strange domestic asceticism, study suspended,
composition constant (yet, somehow, infrequent), quiet routines, adjourned ambition,
yet still some resolve. In such an atmosphere, how to assess what follows?

---

15   See Drowningman, *Rock and Roll Killing Machine* (Huntington Beach, CA: Revelation Records, 2000), LP.

16   See March 24, 2017.

17   Though hardly in surround sound.

These sonnets just… *accumulated*. Over time. One after another. Hyperarchival, parallactic, intoxicating, imperative, these words consume my worst intimations of mortality: raising my hands in twenty-first-century-style desideratum: battering rams of work, work, *work*.[19] I am going to give lessons

in physics. The euphony of warning blanks nomination, accrues deterritorialization, compiles combustion in the lakebed and gouges the revival of all that reading we forgot to do last year.[20] What got "left out"? The hypercontemporaneity of your poorest decisions, the destructive influence of friends, a love story,

every band I ever listened to, religions of redemption, a historical account of capital, a sufficient understanding of difference, a critical confrontation with a new national hate, and other stuff. But perhaps enough about belied absence, the thereness of 2017 affects systematic and engulfing presence. Time's laceration

segments weeks, months, years.[21] Mute, neutral utterances leak through rifts in the SF[22] calendar accommodating our lurch through post-Holocene specimen days laboring mystified on this warming planet, describing the outlines of small lives, limiting the possible outcomes of every single second. More, more

stuff, more weakness, more exhaustion, more toil, more. Memory and woe and mistakes and revision and surrender. All success *turned*, cathected, strategized, vanished. And yet, that was the *project*,[23] the plan, the practice, the days into years, the life into tiny lyric granules, the "experience" into some discernible

form,[24] some judgment, some "meaning," some concrete statement. Oh 2016.[25] You're the scene of a crime, a brutal highway collision, a figure of fascination, a *caesura* in the fabric of historical space-time. Unexpected, your wavering inconstancy infected everything else without mercy. You streamed into the stacks

18   See The Dillinger Escape Plan, 'Destro's Secret," *Calculating Infinity* (Upper Darby, PA: Relapse Records, 1999), LP.

19   "The history of the Species: work, work, work" (John Berryman, "Dream Song 179" [1968], in *Dream Songs* [New York: Farrar, Straus and Giroux, 1969], p. 198, line 16); also see Fifth Harmony, ft. Ty Dolla $ign, "Work from Home," YouTube, February 26, 2016, https://www.youtube.com/watch?v=5GL9JoH4Sws.

20   See Sheila Liming, "In Praise of Not Not Reading," *Point*, April 5, 2017, https://thepointmag.com/2017/criticism/in-praise-of-not-not-reading.

21   Presidential terms.

22   Science and speculative fiction.

23   It was always waiting: on Mabel and Negley, Melwood and Murray.

and anticipated every forthcoming volume. Your intransigency toward any and all other (better, utopian) realities left us without any proper prophets nor competent arbiters.[26] And then you decided not to cease but to keep going. Well, here's at least the beginning of an indictment: putting time on trial, gathering evidence from different invested

witnesses about its calendrical felonies. But it's also, clearly, just an innocent bystander to other much more serious offences. Both subject and object, we then become neither.[27] If a decade ago apprenticeship concluded by contemplating its vanishing, its waste, in 2017 time overwhelms, catastrophically multiplying the incidence of the newness

of the now now,[28] an avocal barrage of novelty rooted in the unsounded depths of pre-digital antiquity, an affective embrace of abstract multidimensional geometry without instrumental duration, parallels to all points of infinity from the singular occasions piling upon one another, obscuring by coalescence

when we might be. Time's lasting attraction[29] collapses my catholic attention, flusters my exuberant referentiality, tasks the circuit boards of memory with too many background applications. It is not just lost or slipping away… time's errant tomfoolery sutures mourning to ecstasy with inveterate motions

of recall and projection. Today slides its weary body through last week and ten thousand years from now. Today abrogates peripheral objects, challenges my constitutional *avidya*[30] to do anything more than flail and cry, impossible. Today concurs with the beginning and end and yet lets slip any boundary.

---

24   See Mark Greif, "The Concept of Experience (The Meaning of Life, Part I)" (2005), in *Against Everything: Essays* (New York: Pantheon, 2016), 77–95.

25   "What can I say about the 'now' of April 2016, as a context within which literature must today be read and taught? . . . The United States is still hell-bent on autoimmune self-destruction" (J. Hillis Miller, "Should We Read or Teach Literature Now?," in *Thinking Literature across Continents*, by Ranjan Ghosh and J. Hillis Miller [Durham, NC: Duke University Press, 2016], 184).

26   Though a welcome and refreshing abundance of critics.

27   "The information revolution and its time bomb are merely the austere revelation of the fi-niteness of the place of history and its tripartite chronology. Which explains the sudden acceleration of common reality these days and the 'excess reality' that subverts our past history—but also the contemporary history of a present rendered inert and inconsequential in the face of the chronotype of an instantaneity that causes us to escape the geo-historic chronotope of everyday activity… Strangely, these days, no one judges it necessary to reconsider our relationship to time" (Paul Virilio, *The Futurism of the Instant: Stop-Eject* [2009], trans. Julie Rose [Malden, MA: Polity, 2010], 92, 99).

28   Now.

Time cannot be wasted but leaves us overtasked by and hopelessly awash in cosmic relations, every point connecting to every other, dispersed, voided, exhausted. Not at the path's culmination—desert forever—but paradisal and abrupt immersion. So for now, done. Arbitrary conclusions, less finished than diffused,

but regardless, *chosen*. We might project certain phenomenological encounters for next time: a wading into the spatial contours of new things. Bodies emerging and contacting, allowing fresh speech, different voices (my own, perhaps). But of course, that will have to *wait*. Yesterday and tomorrow, no longer

an ecstatic incineration but the smoldering embers of postyouth. All the voices that have yet to cohere and spread reflect on dripping in stasis, repeating and differentiating, anticipating their own worlding enunciation—they are about to arrive, singing.[31] Our SF present should not obscure the recent yet still persistent

history upon which megastructures to come will find some purchase (if the logic of dronology can abate). If we are simultaneously and synchronically threaded through some eternally reoccurring multiplicitous *and* solipsistically stranded virtual hypertime of manifold universes, we still only have our annual measures,

our fissionable quantification, our unconditionally permissive temporal structures: 2013, 2014, 2015, 2016 (2017).[32] Beyond, perpetuating, later, different generational folds might promote further *suono*, but here yet another verge has been reached and the divisions might (can we say it?) just happily limn and join certain sympathetic

pulsations. Whatever might retreat, certain encounters and permissible hope have been pedagogically advanced and somewhat more distant horizons beckon. The past's untimely chores disclose the unforeseen. So now now now each entry in the repository only awaits *you*; offered while withdrawing, they document

and respond, some hesitantly, others brashly continuing a dirge begun twenty years ago,[33] but regardless, essaying to deduce a few parameters of the instant and the one after that. So, look to the page's inscription but question its periphery. Perambulate, lay, or sit—on the bus or couch,

29   See Bardo Lièr Parté, *Being and Times* (Oneonta, NY: Freiheit, forthcoming 2018).

30   Ignorance. See Ranjan Ghosh, "Reinventing the Teaching Machine: Looking for a Text in an Indian Classroom," in *Thinking Literature across Continents*, 168.

31   Again, even after preferring not to.

32   Others forthcoming.

in the waiting room—but be wary of the minute's impositions, the loss, the dread. Welcome to years past.[34] They have been preserved and are awaiting your perusal. All the celebrity dead still live here; we can, for a time, synchronize, vibrate, sing. And then, stop. And then.

---

33   See June 1, 1997.
34   If you thought they were irrecoverable, well, some might take issue with such pessimistic historicism.

2017.01: AFTERWORD

/ Bradley J. Fest

And then what next? Can riven speech interrupt our *other* projects?
Despite all, I haven't permitted myself even one minute of nonfiction.[35,36,37,38]
(Because in the hotel room dancing before interviews,[39] I was always just
trying to *read*.[40]) In mid-2017, today,[41] I'll now defer previous tactics for new

strategies, moving ever
so slightly forward while
returning. This may be
toward objects or, *gasp*,
the disorder of nature,
the hysterical acoustic affects
of Earth and all the visible
animals and plants (and people)
and stuff it contains.

Take this cup.

---

35   Let alone nine.

36   Even with all of those quotations.

37   See the "FBI raid" in Annapolis on May 11, 2017.

38   Which, of course, isn't really true.

39   See Daft Punk, ft. Pharrell Williams and Nile Rodgers, "Get Lucky," *Random Access Memories* (New York: Columbia Records, 2013), LP.

40   And what if, seriously, that is somehow now over and I have to inhabit this [redacted] stanzaic space rather than nice easy paragraphs... forever? Well. And then.

41   May 21, 2017.

GAGARIN

/ Louis Armand

c'est fini le temps des poètes
– gil wolman

The Orbital continues like this, night after night. Slant of cosmic rain slashing the blacktop. Dopplered taillights receding. Not alone then. The great migration to outer. Not the sole survivor then. Focus on that. Focus on the drift, the undertow, the invisible line reeling in. A distributed mass of alter egos. Vanishing. And each time around the same again. The same vanishing again. The same slant. The same outer. Till none left. No others left. Only the survival to survive. Repeating. After night: night. Eons of undone time. Focus on that. The second before & the second after. Nothing between. Nothing from nothing, but the random propulsion of an idea. Focus on that. An idea of "nothing." First one, then the other. Gravity's rebirth. The fall. A flashing blue enveloping light.

Gagarin lies there staring at black bits & pieces of retina floating in the light. Do these detached fragments prove Time exists? They watched him. They listened to his thoughts, vital signs. Perhaps the history of a deception isn't the same as the history of an illusion, but what then? If this present moment collapses back into prototype. Winter's painted childhood, the luminous eye wing of a trapped locust. If that moment then was the bow-wave of an orphaned precession. To count at the end as in the beginning. One of these had an author, something intended it. Mind evolving to non-mind. The visor comes down over this floating world. *Know that we come from the sea & are composed of water, which is dialectic.* Space : time : a speck of light. Galactic floes swallowed in the Void, in the Naked Eye dangling from its lifesupport. *Observe this slagged rock on which the great mandala hangs.* All, for the purposes of retelling, diminished to console wraiths, compression artefacts, a faint distant memory of a quantum state. And given a blind coefficient to alter. Gagarin rests at the controls like a stone Buddha contemplating gravity as he/it/they fall upwards into the sky. Choirs & barbaric heliums sing the perfected measure of imperfect things. Under any other conditions this scenario wouldn't be possible. Surrogate, of all that's not to come. And now the cinematically menacing sense that probability knows exactly where he is & when he'll be there. *Man oh man, thou patent anachronism!* Why does he doubt himself. Question mark. "In the moment I'm unaware of myself, do I exist?" An erasure pulsing with capillary life? *The point isn't to preserve memory, but to create it.* The way language creates a horizon from an infinite perspective, converging on two instants separated by a mind the size (93 billion yrs) & age (14 billion yrs) of the cosmos. Brunelleschi by the light of the original photon. To count such evolutionary particulars greater than any whole, would be to expend all foregone conclusions. The lifesupport sends back echoes only. He must learn to decipher them, so as to recognise the enemy when he meets it. That sinful being who is the mind's expression of self-loathing-through-punishment. Nosferatu! Nosferatu in a cumulus of dark matter. *Mon semblable, mon ampère.*

& set out upon a raft through the ill-devised metaphor. *Hurrah for the idiot born from space!*

A rising Vostok in the East. Fiery calligraphy, such stuff as prophesy is made of. Riding the Leviathan into his dankest dreams. The little Oedipus rerun cartoons ringaring in conic sections going round. Daddy stick to glad mammy hole. G-force vertigo turning Borromean knots from his unravelled intestine's pulsing umbilicus. 300 strapped tons of thrust. *Oh Semyorka, my Semyorka!* Ten nine eight seven six. The radios scream. Once more blinded by G.O.D.-light. Ray-Bans & materialist dialectics. Finger-braille clitoris uvula basal ganglia switchboard maniac. Don't shoot the messenger! He's just the meatpuppet tossed from hand to hand. The cremaster in the orgone accumulator. The flyblown ointment. Floating about in the broadcast band like a fish through a film archive. The whole thing's gone autopilot. Electrodes in cortex sing the body electric, zapping a Delgado fix. Technicolor brainspasm comedown. Dostoevsky headsplit. FIRST MANMADE CATASTROPHE IN S=P=A=C=E! The monkey on his back grins, whispers, "If you can do it once, baby, you can do it again & again & again…"

Each cell a perfect hexagon. Assembled into a hive: a geometric eye the remaining dimensions leer through. Was there ever an art distinguishable from judgement? A throw of dice. A bronze cast. *Action enchaîné* in a single defined moment. Europe in its time was a regularly constructed paradox of inexhaustible iteration. They've called him many things. Failed Escape Artist, Gravity's Hostage, Kosmonaut of the Inner Void. To discredit the impossible, in the eyes of such two-dimensional beings as television is made of. Cartoon clowns trip-teasing the world's solemnised radius: Here Dwelleth Dragons, Fringe Elements, Ungovernables. He's the Logos that threatened to get away, brought to heel by a Hero's welcome. Keys to the Kingdom, the Fiefs of Flat Earth, Banlieues of Impenetrable Bureaucracy. They've handed him his lines which now he must hand down to Posterity. Perikles, *The Funeral Oration*. Did Gagarin think he'd even exist if they could've fit a committee in the cockpit? Did they in turn suspect he'd bring the plague down upon them?

Gagarin dreams of Prenatal Life

And so the forward-projective cinema begins. Swimming uphill, the mysteries of oxygen make ruthless advance upon the scenery. Dorsal, vertebra, evolving wing. More sombre variations on the theme of birds. Kino-eye of the flying cinematograph. They're counting the frames in reverse like sleepless auditors, tax consultants, secret agents, resurrection stuntmen leaping midair courtesy of the most blatant camera effects. Their stopwatches are hungry predators flexing their jaws. Already there, always ahead.

Gagarin finds the Enormous Mind inside his head! The last empty landscape, beckoning to enter. The sun inside the cave, an unfolded horizon of cat's eyes & nebulous effigies & shipwrecks. He floats through low-orbit suburban sprawls, industrial estates, zones of drift & boredom. Invisible forces of incessant noise. *History is a trick of light.* The instruments are calculating the number of steps required to recover his initial state. A man alone, shot to pieces, at the end of the road. Silence finally, also unheard.

A voluptuous, forensic victim drowning in the unsleep they've created for him. Desolate angels of release. Mechanics of G.O.D.'s impermeable will. Dreaming of them, always, on the occasions he's allowed to dream. Of the agitated observer, of the immovable father. *Mein Gott, hilf mir, diese tödliche Liebe zu überleben!*

Ridiculous as an emotional commonplace in the mouth of a robot, with all creation raining down. Even the monumental fermi-

ons' erotic petrification, makes a wandering unrest of the Art-
ist's pinhole eyes, diurnal, ambivalent. How nakedly he's served
them. "In this lifetime," they whisper, "desire only a frontier!"

In the family-viewing section, sculptured behemoths became ex-
tinct exactly on schedule. It's a story told through the eyes of
a stenographer for an audience of filing clerks. The task wasn't
to show the truth but to induce in the spectator the belief that
they'd discovered it. Hungry for a sentence that could be pur-
sued to the end with absolute certainty – of a word as definitive
as a tombstone – of a book after which nothing more can be
said.

Neither this nor the next world, but in a polysemy of circulation.
The end isn't the end, there was no beginning. (Escape, always
by retrospective.) *Pourquoi pas un petit jeu de mots ma chérie?*
Cleansed of the odour of veneration, the question about the
basis of Art now begins to find an answer.

The View Back

Was there something prior to this nonexistence? If finally
to be translated from the language he was born in to the one in
which everything passes away. Glint in the eye of the Artist he
dreams is dreaming him. Yuri Alekseyevich Gagarin. Embryo of
the life to come. Path through territories unknown. Uncom-
passed. To attempt an account would be a fool's errand. But a
fool wouldn't flinch, only an idiot in love with the Higher Vani-
ties.

Gagarin the fearless alienist ascended the orgone accelerometer. "To the weird future!"

008 In-Flight "Vostok" April 12, 1961. Let's go! (*Cockpit noise. Overload vibes. Tubular bells with blast-off feedback.*) All systems quadraphonic. Roger that. You're coming through, G-man. Mama mama! Ride that babushka! Oh she feels great! A-wop-bop-a-loo-bop! Blow blow blow! I'm the big bazooka with the megaton beluga! Slap me a Khrushchev! Cram Castro up the Guadalcanal! I'm Che Guevara's hotrod Harley! Tesla's tonne-up turbo thruster! Lee Harvey's magic supersonic peashooter right through John F Kennedy's brain! Ho ho ho! I do the Marilyn Monroe demerol-in-the-arse you fucken yankee trash! Move over Savonarola! Shift the gears up! We're going straight to the top! King of the heap! Kong of the cosmo-kebab! El Mucho Mas Enchilada! Gonna plant my hammer&sickle right in the sky! Hey suckers, eat my second stage separation! I'm burning you up! You gettin' this loud & clear? I'm sticking my red star in yr spangled bazooma! Well looky here, mum! Ee dat de Oit doun dere troo da poithole winda? Ooh aint she pretty as a peepshow! All spread out wiv er big fat Mississippi! Got them Deltoid Blues, coz I aint woke up yet, hehehe, but I aint dreamin of you, Polly Maggoo! What ho? Sea ahoy! U-boats! Torpedoes! Blitzkrieg! Down down down goes the clash of the Titanic! See the vast Ice Ages of Niemansland re-arise! Nightbomber Neanderthals chilled on Nembutal! Auroras! Sibelian tundras! Malevich! Kandinsky! Hans Arp! RKO! Electric archangels vault the North Pole! And here comes the Tsar Bomba matinee triple-bill! Powering up the supadoopa third stage now! Oh what a blast! A great pyrocumulus! A Walt Disney nimbostratus! A psilocybin psychosolaris! Schön, schöner, am schönsten! Mother Russia lies with arms out weeping smiling laughing her head off! I launch myself upon that vast bosom! That tumultuous heaving mass! Rivers, factories, terrains, power stations, snowdomes, kosmodromes, Stalingrads, gulag archipelagos! A whole Pathé newsreel unspooling down there! I wave out my window & the whole of future humanity waves back! A weightless tear floats from my eye! But this is no time for nauseating sentimentality! I see the horizon coming up! Mene, mene, shadows upon the

Face of the Void! The vision fades! Sky! Black! Black sky! I'm passing beyond History into the unknown! Into the unknown! Into the unknown! (*Tape reaches the limit switch.*)

& thus G.O.D. created Gagarin female & male, aerial & earthly, immediate & intermediate, logos & sigil, trance & labyrinth, Odyssey & Iliad, cyberial & diurnal, agnostic & speculative, superfluous & trigonometric, hidden hand & conspicuous cumshot, telepresent & nebulous, terminal-head & exoskeleton, resonant entity & resonant evolver, ghost in the machine & human patsy, eyebeam & crosshair, action without intention & action intended remotely, Big Time & Hilbert space, tumbrel & metamitic, Jill & Jack, chondrule & helium thread, hyperbolic & catachrestic, hieroglyphicist & No Logo, a stitch in time & a stent in the coronary artery, base & superstructure, state & recovery, the eros of sea-hair & the cadence of carriage returns, solitary & innumerate, legendary & unspeakable, bride of Gaia & bard of Panopticon, drift & boredom, anal & rectal, signifying monkey & commodity fetish, pervitin & belespon, vernal & equinox, the sphere of circulation & the domain of logistics, Hegel & Kant, stim-bot & time bomb, manic & depressive, Sotadic obscenity & obsolescent sapience, riot cop & truncheon, a bird in the hand & $\sqrt{2}$ in the bush, erectile & molluscan, action in reaction & irreversible entropy, inside & outside, sound booth & echo chamber, autochthonous & automaton, absolute zero & the nth degree, erasure & inscription, short straw & long straw, symbiotic & symbolic, tête-bêche & sixty-nine, the moment before & the instant after, dualism & binary, replication & dissipation, diabolic & diastolic, substance & hyperstance, source code & sauce bottle, exile & wilderness, the word known to all men & its fatally fatuous enunciation, 12-tone scale & total eclipse, helix & bottleneck, haplessness & happenstance, the way home & the longest way round, mantrap & wombfruit, clearing house & central ledger, the categorical cart & connotative horse, the way of the world & a world away, montage & remonstrance, image macro & deep fake, switchboard & synaesthesia, mutoid & equivocation, the value of paying attention & the abstract purity of verbal kitsch, sense & sensibility, elevator musak & waiting-room Pantone schemes, hard rain & acid noir, retrorocket &

avantgarde, perineum & perihelion, stance & counter-stance, objective correlative & elective affinity, cyclic redundancy & vicious circle, variable A & variable B, all & nothing, blah & blah...

Speak or be silent! The diligent thought police perform their checklist for the nth occasion. To observe the observed. To unperform the prescribed function. Darkmatter inflates peripheral. Industrial meat factories match the horizon step for step. Dead seas churned by dead waves. Vacuum sealed. Is this the Future he was programmed to long for? Transistored, rosycheeked sweating oratories of collateral affect? Data-aggregates to virgin his bedsheets? A state funeral? The unctuous Frankensteins who populate his sleep, flipping the switches. The Evel Knievel act, the Houdini routine, the Human Cannonball. Piloting his thoughts by remote control like crematoria at terminal velocity. The eye by which the world sees him isn't the eye by which he sees it. Extinction Harbinger! Man in the Resurrection-Machine! Creature from Beyond! Is transcendence this? A cry of pain in a throat parched beyond repair? Love in austere times? Perhaps the misplaced original voice-recording. Blackboxed. Johnny Cash in a microwave oven, breathing an atmosphere of pure ignited oxygen. To be a piece of molten meteorite imploding through undimensioned timespace: the inscribed singularity, in embryo, of the long-lost Cosmic Unconscious. For nothing if not to dream audaciously. Or not at all.

There are worlds where the sea never makes landfall. To drown must be a horrible thing.

Casting off into the day's blight. Cityscapes in rain or hail — move often. The very idea of a bridge. Alphabetic fire escapes on Harlem tenements. Vapour trails spiralling into wet sidewalks. There is no paraphrasable meaning. The urge to outer of the averted beyond. Riding a Brooklyn-bound A-train to stare at the Atlantic, imagining others on the far side staring hatefully back. Erosion gradually of everything to microplastics swept back&forth across ocean floors. Smog-mute leviathans of dusk presage entropy. Switch channels & it's night again then day & the debated obvious. Whose time is always now. Knowing the war will never end. Never be over. G.O.D. wasn't the first maniac at home in this century. "I am the hand erasing the dust," Quasimodo says. Still waiting for the hour when machines clock-off & a voice through the floor bringing the glad tidings. "At least we'll laugh before midnight," say Marlene Dietrich's legs. The past watched over them while they slept. Libraries of ant-people adept at removing incongruous dandruff. *Whole Iliads stretched out from Piraeus without you in mind.* "A longer way to go," they jeered, "a lot less to lose." Evil from imposing good on others, the sacrificial ritual of writing (Tsvetaeva): "Who sees injustice in the fact my hands are raw?"The Tao says, *The way that can be described isn't the true way.* Gagarin! Hung from a chandelier with his defeat still growing inside him – beyond the world where complaining isn't permitted. "There're many who pretend that cannons are aimed at them, when in reality they're the target merely of opera glasses" (Brecht). And though it has many eyes some of them must sleep – intoxicated by acid rainfall & beautiful sinking ships & all tomorrow's just conditions. Telling of how, in a ball floating over the equator, the desert never fails to return. First, the letters dim, an oasis of light makes solitudes Rembrandtesque: nations of self-haters posed with walking sticks, though the writing on the wall cld be ancient Egyptian. Deft of touch, you cause things to move that aren't there. Always blood on someone else's hands. Out in the initial oceans, they are humourless, unafraid of ridicule, those mythic beasts. No arms, legs, bones to break. Picking the scabs three days late when they came to bury him. And lay on the linoleum with tiny abjects in his mouth, "playacting." Where next? After the Shangri-la years, the Rubber Man act. Eichmann in Jerusalem, the Beatles, Minuteman, Bay of Pigs. Earth was drowning at gunpoint, in a swimming pool painted black. Vast TV wastelands. Another professional loser on a comeback streak, another treadmill-with-rat, Dostoyevsky in queerface. Progress report: *The life of my body I fail to cultivate, the body I was born with & not some strap-on placebo?* Solzhenitsyn was quiet at lunch, Pasternak hanged himself: carried someone's head around in a suitcase for years before they caught him jaywalking – nailed his feet to the ceiling & his collar to his chest. Such are the timely intercessions of right reason applied to practice. Leaves blow across doorsteps & Gagarin is brought closest to things that vanish. Yesterday Berlin & jetlag, tomorrow a vaulting Nureyev to the Moon. Falling away to Nevsky Prospekt & harbour sounds & static drifting over the bridge. Approximately 66 million names disappeared from the public record. Ahead of their time in a world that'll always be too late. Their G.O.D. was primitive space technology. Before the war, after the war. There were occasions when he never wanted to leave. We've all been there at one time or another, flat-footed through the outerspace of the suburbs, erecting a steadfast irrelevance. The giant camera in the sky, thought balloons, a single origin. But these wandering lights are not the cynosure, they are the product of dead ends where many languages spoke. Even the most fervent is a temporary ziggurat, a showerhead talking from Venus, haemoglobins of deep spiritual intent. Like watching his hair fall out. The eyes: two orbiting Sargassos in which all the cartoon backwash drifts. Because Gagarin, too, is an interpenetrated being, his makers regale him with plastic fruit. Plutoniums & barbaric heliums. Each time the world hangs in the balance – like clockwork all the beautiful ideas lie blushing in a field of stones. Strawmen sobbing into the public breast – crows in the clouds – the orphanage on the hill. Picture a landscape in which no one's buried. Escape wld be as pedantic as archaeology turned to a cinema of durations. Switch channels & a staged moonrocket teeters in the sky, sublime as an angular momentum couched in rhyme or blood-laughter interjected with all the summary gravitas of Heinrich Himmler doing the Resurrection Cakewalk. Safe, he thought, for the time being. They came, they departed: their traces are everywhere but we are learning to erase them. Weightlessness, too, has something in common with thought. If you throw a stone, the stone transmits its image: the question is, does it suffer? 60 years ago they'd've had a pump organ for a soundscape – the secret agent studying his photograph by torchlight, Paris on strike, the betrayed backtrack. His aura came out in the wash with the rest of History, like "The Star-Spangled Banner" in an aqualung, deaf to the world. The opposite cld equally be true – shouting down the line or punching through space (language being also disinformation): in a window with no one blocking the view, as open as a ravine y're too busy falling into to suspect till it's too late. The whole fiasco cld be watched, the way a gratuitously rained-on scenery is, or a dog, or a whining gear. Stooping under the world's weight, stations of the meteorological cross in windswept *agitato furioso*, the sea nothing but tormented metaphor? He looked furtively back but the road was gone, only a mountain path winding away like the sliced white underbelly of something. A 5 A.M. emetic – lancing the cyst on a pineal egg, a hagfish's eye – but an intelligent species needn't tell itself that it is. There are actions never intended for repetition: what are they for? Gagarin breathes, in a compulsive, formulated rhythm, propelled by a type of resemblance. A photographic emulsion, a baptism. Though the days of pilgrimage are over. Though the tedious enumerations exist only to be immemorial. Frontiers of contraband make a Rushmore in the distant sky – hitchhiking to Hollywood to live the late-night movie, $4 suitcase & street-corner pointed shoes. All the Yellow Brick Roads running to landfill. Postcards of the Anthropocene. The future was all TV reruns. It was a hard act to follow, a bum note to riff, a rough coat to wear – all the misunderstood answering machines crying themselves to sleep. Hello, is it over yet? At first they didn't see it approach: "It's dark," they said, inaudible but we needn't hear them to guess their dilemma. Its horns gouge the air – catalyst, oracle, & not the least retiring thing. "Power's never ridiculous," said the dumbwaiter disguised as Joséphine Bonaparte's breasts – he twists spoons with his eyes, cocktail onions & autisms. Anything for a laugh. What the tribe demands is magically provided, in happy dreamlike hours that're meanders of dust as upon some quantum littoral. Are these the suicide bombers we've long suspected? Furtively the baize parts to outlined rotogravure, of stockings on ladders, of unwindable clocks. Chained in the dark the hung meat turned inexorably whiter. Still Gagarin awoke screaming.

Black. River. Voice. Antennae. Windwhipped. Windlashed. Pitchforked. In the night-transmission control room they've mind-sized every last word into amorously collaged nonsense. Photocelled in brain-lozenge. Trees festooned with dead cathode. The cosmic baobab. *And I an ant in a baobab fruit, tossed on Fibonacci seas.* One desperate spiralling attempt at mentalised Hindu-Arabic. It was lightyears till they understood, every account begins with a great white zero crowding the sky. "What the hell have I seen?" He spins he spins he spins through the paranoid microdimensions. The hands forget their contrapuntal. Switch. Valve. Bivalve. This driving perplex. Eyemute. The spill of it. Damned-up in a hurled surrounding. Every streetlight implodes to bodyweight. At last. Finally free to fall. Out of the tree lying upright. Femur. Tibia. Arise & walk, the voices said. Ungainly as naked lifesupport. Face-mumbling thyroid resonances. Mutoid word-loops layered, detuned. They expect him to swing down out of his wombhole Tarzan-like for the camera crews. Audiotronics at full throttle, the evolved vocal cord. How often had they rehearsed this bit? Expecting him to ape his lines badly or too well. Generations of ratings-stunt worship failing to repair. Or light to reappear. Sucked like canned applause back through entropy's clockwork. To re-affect. Each emotive first step as cold-blooded as the last. Each last unresembling the first. He'd learn only how to repeat, a thousand times over. Sleepless in the mirror of himself. *Enemy, I am you. I've always been you.*

Darkness falls from the air. (Having witnessed everything, it was time to move on.)

Aggregated into time, the traps learnt to scent you before they're set. A room inside an echo, a rude observation post hand-worked like an original UFO. Progress, its very blankness implies it. *The same tendencies in Enlightenment philosophy: the mathematical modes of human understanding, the absolute opposition of subject & object, & the conception of truth as unchanging.* There was to be no more depiction – people had died for less. Lying there with the vapid eroticism of a détourned prodigal, telling you there *is no war.* In the nebulous cave, strange fruit hangs from an insubstantial threat, resolutely *tabula rasa.* Just as Damascus is far from where *it* seems – even the walls of its irreducible reality are TV static. 40,000 Years of Modern Art. How late still to be counted as having arrived – & now the silos, too, gaping omnivorous & starved at the sky like a lost Golden Age. There's always more pathos in denial – Europe in 1945, the first conquistador, Carthage after rain. Instructed "not to

give in," things wldn't be different with a shared point-of-view
– the children he'd been spying on all winter, taking their game
behind doors to inner soviets of the mind's eye. Deliberately
the finger hesitates over the switch, awaiting the signal for the
ominous coincidence to occur.

With respect to the spatio-temporal dimensions:
the dimensions of an object are observer-dependent;
an object's scale is relative to the measuring device: for an infin-
itesimally small measuring device, the dimensions of the object
are infinite & vice versa;
a dimension is therefore the persistence of an observable value
over time yet liable to change in its conditions of observation;
dimensions are contiguous "incommensurables" & are not ex-
trinsic to observation but conditional for it;
the erroneous object is also real.

And they are wondering how Spring comes. Flag-waving
handpuppets mining the foundations, wolfwhistle a vagueless
Anatolia of glass terrains, no Chekhovian seagulls out here as
dusk indicates. Farsighted by the very nature of their craft, yes-
terday many targets liquidated. The language of edicts makes
novelisation moot. Terse shrinkwrapper intone of product envy,
wire-rimmed, nothing to be exploited here. To silence Cinder-
ella's carbuncular foot-fetishist, the dreamware climbed out of
his head & stomped him to death. Naturally there's no abid-
ing. Street-sharman with ear to faintly tolling stones. In lock-
step the wind comes out of nowhere a roaring Narcissus. All
nominalistic proof is useless: *je mangerais ma merde* Arthur Cra-
van. Measures drastically blank respiring in chrysalis. Footsteps
into thin air give picturesque weather its content, a front-row
wrestling of integrals, angles, conic sections. By reason alone he
could stand a rocket on its head. Flowering excrements of er-
ror or juxtapose. Stop. Back in the lucky place, glorious battles
were fought for wars that'd ended, truces cheered for wars that
hadn't. Pingpong between the margins, all the fumes of sur-
rounding incense with which you make love to planets from
afar. Every clue is a new line delivering messages to an imbecile
with a backpeddle brake. Drowned at the bottom of the space-

ship operating manual, one finds what one looks for.

The protagonist has stepped off into space. The protagonist is a hero of the people. The protagonist is beyond reach. The protagonist is the future. The protagonist demonstrates the success of the Five-Year Plan. The protagonist is functioning normally. The protagonist has been subjected to strenuous testing. The protagonist catches the ball. The protagonist is nothing special. The protagonist eats three times a day. The protagonist sits in the chair. The protagonist is ready for use. The protagonist has exhibited reactionary tendencies. The protagonist has a momentum equal to mass times velocity squared. The protagonist cares what you think. The protagonist is a myth. The protagonist has a standard daily protein intake. The protagonist is happy. The protagonist is aware of its insignificance. The protagonist says hello. The protagonist sleeps in your bed when y're not there. The protagonist knows what you don't know. The protagonist is too good to be true. The protagonist prefers blondes. The protagonist has committed suicide. The protagonist executes the correct subroutine as scheduled. The protagonist offers false hope. The protagonist is satisfied if you are. The status of the protagonist is equivalent to a blank transmission. The protagonist is fully operative. The protagonist is G.O.D.'s messenger. Each protagonist comes with a failsafe. The protagonist is one-in-a-million. The protagonist answers for its actions. The protagonist is raining. The protagonist wishes you many happy returns. The protagonist is lonely. The protagonist was invented for the purpose of deceiving the enemy. The protagonist awaits yr command. The protagonist falls mainly on the plain. The protagonist is a ghost in spectral time-delay. The protagonist is equivocal. The protagonist has ejected from the module. The protagonist demonstrates the value of paying attention. The protagonist is out of joint. The protagonist has a number of options available to it. The protagonist dreams of itself dreaming of itself. The protagonist is a thing. The protagonist describes a set of probable observations. The protagonist is a figment of mass hysteria. The protagonist's circuit is dead. The protagonist is not the protagonist.

In search of nothing his efforts resulted in Art. A sea of
lice in the control module, a desert ringed by plague, ghosts in
advance formation of space junk, comsats, ICBMs. Through his
dialectical-subjective periscope, Gagarin observed the rescue
ship with its delicate cargo sink under the hydrometrics of the
last glacier. These were blueprints for ending: bonesounds small
& portable or large being the chief characteristic. Throughout
the 20th century those possessing aura took on the mantle of
fabrication, the preparation of glue from bones for example.
Transponders radars conical middens of fissile junk. A ship-
wreck on the moon the only place not impossible for future Art
to survive? A blackhole in place of the camera-eye serves as a
protagonist in the absence of any other.

**Seeing from memory the familiar false witnesses one or
two with files in metal boxes.** Their manifesto glued on
canvas found in flea markets. In the final analysis, two zeroes in
the pursuit of separation. The word appears in its elementary
form, the necessity of life, by means of value-relations. Ear-
blind. Wet mouth on wet skin. Mouth turned inside out as if
a wet latex glove. As if a scream were a laugh turned inside
out. The colorectal cancer of the mind-eye located by what can
be seen & what can't. Floating there in its orbit *à la* digital-
compression artefacts. Resonant. Becoming the object it d(en)
ominates. Neckshackled. Airlocked. Nerve-mesh. The voice of
an anatomical dictionary. Index of sigils. Dejected creations
perversely iterate on every page. *I who raise my fist, which doesn't
belong to me.* Employed in grey areas to ameliorate unshakeable
conviction. World-within-vaselined-world. A steel ball pum-
melled by hostile force. Among the dancing holograms. The si-
lent typographies of dread. The weather, the factories, the TV
news. Awe-shocked in his epileptic's periscope. A light in the
sky. Mirror to an audience of braille-readers supposed to be
watching the watchers. Supposed. To be. Watching. The watch-
ers.

Art must place unreasonable demands. Worlds fall apart
each instant in a sliding equilibrium. There are things an artist
shouldn't know. Untenable constructions during the course of

the night – the hidden spectacle of wave-function collapse – an erotics of vanishing. In short, art could almost not exist. But there is more to stupidity than meets the eye.

A speck rests in the corner he'd like to brush away but can't. *Un bel niente.* Oranges on a blue&white tablecloth. Landscape with people inked into the distance, diagram-like. All the middle-grounded variants on an indecisive theme the Artist, a giant in smeared apron, stoops over to complete or re-erase or elaborate into a truth that resides in the reality of appearance. Or unappearance. Or the unforeseen. And the light that produces it, merged against its will into inseparable being. *Credo in unum.* A world no less, to evolve & be snuffed out (like two mutually opposed yet ramifying hemispheres, locked in carnivorous struggle)? You'd take the measure of him in a Troy weight – standing at the triple-point of himself, in its green & naked appearance. And what art! The audience withholds its applause like a portentously mixed metaphor. Rotely performing its judgements, its mind-hydraulics. An austral compass with no guiding points but the frozen eyes in which it drifts – faces with mouths – grey fossil bodies on a seabed. A *casse-tête*… They've become the essence of it. Perhaps it reminds of that recurring dream in which his dead mother is dutifully standing on her head in the doorway, telling about the pain of paralysis – & how there were frozen pipes all through winter & no one had loved her as they ought to. And kept her foetuses in the microwave for posterity. The Artist squats in the corner laughing. "Look," he roars, "they even talk!" Though the words are a fly-covered pulp – like plangent apocryphal first fruits. He'll smudge his thumb across Gagarin's forehead & the miracle will repair contrariwise: he'll be the drowned coxswain, or the sentry keeping always on the alert to observe what takes place, or the Wandering Jew, or Švejk, or Josef K, or Ruy López de Segura, or Alekhine in an Odessa prison cell teaching Lev Trotsky the moves… The kind of man who goes a long way towards self-explaining. You switch on a light, it's simple: the counterforce of a finger on a smooth expanse – the incorporated error – gravity's in-curve to unscaled approximation. "Life," he'll tell you, "isn't the exact science art is." Like rain, it impinges. And in the picture, too, it's raining, coming over the rooftops in a faintly fingered fretboard movement. It soothes & distracts. The flagstones glisten like geometries awaiting rediscovery – & Gagarin also is waiting, beside the greyblack monument with walled horizons drawn in on a space that makes a contracting lung of itself, starved of oxygen. He's Jan Hus & they're building a fire at his back, its flames leap as the waters lap, quid pro quo. He's the glint in a movie-camera eye – a polychrome of scripted intimations gaslighting the native ego – the midget hauling operatic stage scenery on its back – an oracle of the next Palmyra: *une table, des chaises, un canapé, une fusillade*. Dürer's skull lies on a desk, exhibit A. Times being what they are, Gagarin too will take all he can get. Trying not to see the pattern of his crimes, the ratings snuff-job, the evidence sent up in funerary smoke as offering to perturbed heavens tilted on a thirty-million-year axis. The journey begins at starting points not of his choosing – marooned in this middle & precarious place, like a wo/man drawn & quartered on a pedestal. To be hung in a foursquare gibbet or wheeled in a cage across pantomime seas where neoprimitives poke quizzing glasses at his effigy & everyone's drunk. The simpering Picasso-eyed gorgons, the three-piece hymenoptera careering like dumb entities they harvest to light empty office space – *très atmosphérique*. The moment stakes everything or barely one thing. A door closes. Did Gagarin speak before he was gone, saying what he saw? Gnarl of fist & gnarled eye? Who's the uncanny guest knocking at the one available window? Shadows creep up the walls: it was a dream, he said – like Blas Roca who shined shoes before bedding down in the presidential palace – & he said, *When I die, cover me in leaves & bury me under the mango tree by the house on the junction*. It was the tree he used to sit & think under – but instead they put him in a fancy mausoleum at El Cacahual with the Party faithful. And now he waits for the Revolution & Amerika both to crumble like pyramids on the Usumacinta, with howler monkeys & mosquitoes & mango trees. Who says justice isn't deserved? Gagarin's effigy gazes down upon the equator as it spools & unspools in time-delay. Painting the scene backwards from the dominant myth at the empty centre of the world in single-point perspective. The Artist readjusts him so as to take it all in, the vanishing panorama, the parrots in the trees. "And if wishes were horses?"

he says, turning the picture on its side, thereby completing it.

In his dream he is walking & walking through the cosmic rain. A pair of cheap plastic shoes with the soles ridged & holed & drainwater fizzing out the seams till they flap apart & he's stuck barefoot halfway across the city. The bridge. The river. The night-heron diving down through black water like cosmonauts with severed lifelines rippling the wake.

I knew early on that I was quite unique. A spinning *corps de ballet* head then feet then head now Africa now the horizon then a cloud of fire in the sky. *I waited for separation. There was none. I knew I was dead. They put a stand-in in my head.* The wrong eye in the wrong orbit. Camera fusillade, extrication anguish, sex with robots. Only a madman hears dogs barking in space. They'd been rivals from an early age, his alter ego's alter ego. *Heaven is a dentist's waiting room tortured by subliminal musak.* It was the opposite of everything they'd been taught to expect: the weather below, the lights rushing days-per-hour per-minute per-blink-of-the-eye. All the Zone clocks turn obediently in reverse. Image macro, view-finder, the salient meme in the embrace of the world. *History is a suspended animus* (it was the last observation he recorded, before erasing that too). He was the patsy in a mission that existed only in the mind of a man visible to everyone. Immobile, fixated, bound. If he stares through the glass hard enough will Gagarin see G.O.D.? Not knowing which reflections will move with him & which without. Quixote tilting at the equinox, an aberration of starlight, a mock of paracelene? Their hypertrophic exit strategies had a brittle edge, harnessed to art's malign sleeplessness. And would he play surrogate in turn to *his* contrary? Celestial music crept upon his cortex like an unread autopsy report: *This durée ends that others may begin.* Immaculately born from the kosmonaut's head, did the invisible Artist watch over him like a compassionate golem? The drone sky, the picture-machine's hidden hand casting elongated shadows? For 108 minutes the criminogenic escape artist dreams he's free, before dissolving into airlessness. They are waiting with their butterfly net to catch him when he falls. The replicant who slipped up, asleep at the wheel, deprogrammed by the control panel's chant. The playlist reveals: 1. Rondo for Orbiting Bodies in a Multiple Tempo. 2. Stereotypes for Landing Pad & Reverse Countdown. 3. Combustion Economies Snowballing through Hell. Gagarin's heard it all already, heard it all, in his implanted *déjà vu.* Only a lunatic wouldn't be paranoid about what their talking pictures had in store. He's got the whole world under surveillance, but all eyes are on him. *You think there's some way outa this, kidz?* Playing the hemispheres like a schizophrenic theremin. The erupting echo chamber blossoming into nova: onyx-veined, a psychic melanoma. The giant crab's mechanical claw reaches from its isthmus of floating shellac to tickle him under the chin. Night seeps across the Soviets, the Reichs, the mesas, steppes, tundras & atolls, melting & glaciating. Superposition – collapse – superposition. They could deepfake the cosmos if they put their minds to it. Aneurism, dive-bomber, fallen angel, asteroid. He was the *force majeur* of an impossible idea, a glitch in time, an Achilles heel roped to a pulsing umbilicus. The production line's Self-Made Man. The camera's amour. What would it matter if he was mad?

Crumbs fall from the high table. Picked bones. There're always others to take the Master's place. In the village to which he rarely returns. In the Space Museum under the sea. A technician's nostalgia for light switches, secret checklists. In the morning the enemy was defeated. Defeated. Defeated. Heavy objects piled upon their absurd names. There is no native tongue, only the voice of the ALL. Spiralling in a sublime transitory accomplishment. Sub-luminal masses on the cusp of velocity. Baikonur. Moscow. Berlin. Prague. Kiev. Belgrade. Tallinn. Peenemünde. Vladivostok. Time at a standstill. Anxiety lies in wait under breathable atmospheres to crush the bones in the skull, eject marrow like rancid toothpaste. Coming back from the cinema after midnight, the stars did shine.

Altogether their vast accomplishment equalled an intimate uproar in a china cup. An animal orchestra. A Heidelberg jawbone, an angry penguin with a ruined shirtfront. Drawn with all the force of its indeterminacy, the spilt milk belies an air of excessive formalism – each mark in its specific orbit like a moon or an egg of tranquil lunacy balanced on a spoon. A point on a line between *nude* & *sleep*. There are gothic underground parking lots with which he feels affinities. Dimorphic, eutherian, as alien hands that shape a vestige of what they'd grasp. Comforting as a café-table Colosseum – the gladiatorial voice, the baffled creatures stalking in retreat to nursery rhymes & Black Forest cake. A raisin-eyed fingerling pricks him with its tusk & in a split second everything tastes like the burnt roof of a mouth or gum arabic, & the special occasions all stared glumly back.

Descartes' dog buries its bone in yr chair, every night when y're not looking (10 theses):

1. In which the Artist considers his resemblance to Melmoth. A torso on the moon, in a fine light slanted – three / tired / parallel / lines where the contradictions lay subtly upon. And laughed, "I am as a tidelocked sea. Not all that can be said, will be." Still at the bedside before his time, & pulls faces in the mirror – "Take up the roles, haha, tear the photographs, the dreadful imaginaries!" *Dancing in the inshala-la, dancing in the...* For the eyes to unclose, for the fear not to. As near as the other side of that window, as History – so long as there's blood in these veins, even if other people's. He considers his resemblance.

2. Looked at verbwise in unpolished glass as "from within" the picture resembles in its scale & attack a propensity, a notation of mentalese. Arrayed like Saturn's rings, the migraine stirs – strange transits which in ten, a thousand years might still conjunct, luminesce – brain volume & eye volume, the tipped balance. And are our children thus dead before us?

3. He had only two wishes: (x) NOT TO REMEMBER HIS DREAMS, & (y) NOT TO DREAM.

4. The visible light slowed to a standstill, beguiled by the striped wallpaper, *une paysage dépassé*. Watching them wheel their chairs around the park: he only OD'd for the camera, "It's not like y'd make a career of it." Counting black sheep to surface – two pisshole eyes in the correctional high tower. Europe at 3 o'clock in the afternoon was a fish a rock a shit a deletion – "I killed them y're killing me you also must die." Time, if the world turned on a pin, restless in lockstep. And stood behind himself, a ruin –

dead roaches in his hair – conducting the scenery.

5. He concluded on a sour note. He abjured prostituted ached. He confused himself with his avatars. He forgot his hearing.

6. Such a weight borne down for the last stroke – the changeling prince in the bearded-lady pietà *Vergine madre, figlia del tuo figlio...* Lies there in his hand-me-downs while the Weegee politburo guy solemnly pulls a trick from his sleeve for Realism's children to gawk at. But the hand we see in the picture isn't the same as the hand that performs our nightly eviscerations – miming a beat-up transvestite in a Buonarotti clown car. A curtain twitches in the stepped fortress of the hero's mind, as clouds cross the glass left-to-right, forever seaward, & the clock, unadmonished, strikes.

7. All things retrospective by appointment. For instance, who were you? Soulless as the production of uniform opinion is, in the present case, etc. Kind, they said, to ants, flywheels & dust, but a fossil for a backbone. *Ah, how sweet it tastes, the life before they made you.* Four legs because intended to crawl. And hunched beneath a viaduct baying, *Doggerel's death to the dog!*

8. That it creates the myth of itself – the end of the road of the centuries to come, mollusc-eyed – a foetus on a collapsed stretch of paper, crossed out & re-begun – wheels, larvae, ectoplasm – a whole masticated alphabet of choked frenzies. How read the map of this masquerade? The wall-people, the starers, made Sleeping Beauty faces on the TV of his mind; his formative years, dabbling in blank austerities (his face was his revenge).

9. The machine kept everything to schedule – a wind rose through its bones like a vast antipode: dig as they might, the grim adjustments, the dead batteries, weren't cathedrals in space. Nothing here for the opinionated monkeys. Such crimes, such abominations! Omission had always been his intimate companion – he carried a window with him everywhere even on his wedding night (the sperm counts of the galaxies supplicated themselves).

10. He roared, he conjured, he was the century's unacknowledged primitive, vaulting between abyss & nothing – the world-that-begins & the world-without-beginning – to gravitate, as do the parts of the mind, in a mobile epilepsy (that a dog be greater than the sum of its dross?). He was the deuce inside – straining at a gnat & swallowing a camel – the maggot in the brain, the

tightrope-walker with a peg leg. Had they wanted him to exist (to creature the myth of themselves) he'd've refused on principle – he only went where he wasn't welcome.

The search for anonymity began with television. Electromagnetic tides of Gagarinmania. He is forever walking across the gantry, being strapped into the module, parachuting to the ground. He is forever waving at the crowd in Red Square. He is forever sitting at a window staring into empty space. *Not one star in the sky.* Exploding in replay. He could still dream of the moon. A light at the end. The long excruciating corridors leading back to childhood's demise, believing everything prepared for *this*. From guidance system to download history, room temperature, the dictatorship of the fait accompli. Art has a way of being underwhelming: test actions that perform themselves to be not seen. "I" is an experiment with the reader like staring at a screen with green dots (were there green dots in outer space?). It wasn't the first occasion he'd found solace in underground long-term parking. Once more the inexplicable nightmares have returned. Their habits were called "saturation habits," panoptical algorithms, the godmachine at the Schwarzschild Radius: time turns to spaghetti before its eyes. EARTH CAPTURED BY TECHNOCAPITAL SINGULARITY. And Gagarin? Vespucci of lunar incontinence – how long before his diabolical plan is hatched?

Fairly soon the fog will clear – the abandoned countryside, the jutting balconies, the prehistoric rock pictures. Ambivalent volumetric mouth forming a concentric target. Far simpler than it seemed, once there were no more unbearable songs to play on the Inflight Entertainment System. Driving through a night familiar from black&white TV reruns, the fusion sequence with page numbers memorised: as an example of what they had to avoid (mouth, tonsils, larynx) it was world-standard. But how far could it go? Stomaphobia just seemed like congenital misery unless you got it cut out in time – a beggar's opera with hyphens pedantically lodged in the supine semicolon. Equally there was no light in which to receive instructions: was that normal in a case like this? Porous & rocklike, the unexpected rigours of a censored line: you could make a joke out of it. In Technicolor, the key to the collective insoluble dream – & now we have to hear all about the Artist's intestinal complaint. The lymphatic brain, unfound for centuries, began showing up emphatically in all the queerest places. A pair of at-first-glance enamelled eyes, an embryonic gill-slit, a half-coloured mermaid in a child's doodle-book. The Central Committee ordered the nonintersecting timeframes to intersect – do they deserve such scorn? Do you? Another unseasonal storm over Asia Minor turning everything grey. Behind the *Fall of the House of Usher*, the hidden animations failed to erupt on cue: mantle plume of videogenic mouth-phobia. These were to be trusted less than usual, beginning again a career of slipping out unseen from adjacent situations. Whose martyrology are we composing *maintenant*, Monsieur Artaud? As an instance of what, pitched inside its breath, isn't a voice, the expired celluloid cast shadows of doubt on the denuded mouth as the child kissed it. The entire police force looked inside to see if there was anyone still alive in there – joyous as an ochre sky crucified on spears of dusking light. When nothing was left to eat he retired to write his long-awaited manifesto – it was the moment the aliens chose to invade, scaling a state-of-the-art periscope from the Great Crevasse, armed to the teeth with archetypes. "We are among you," the chalked semaphore on the child's doorstep said. Spacemen in mail-order plastic sachets, all they required was the addition of water, oceans of it. Years later, listening to rain on foreign windowsills at night: each time he opened his mouth, innocents suffered. Eventually the censors would be forced to break cover & act "in the public good" – Laurel&Hardy figures making choreographed footprints on the moon, planting G.O.D.'s own flag for TV proletariats grown addicted to advertising. Impaired by amorousness, wheeled creatures disported in the streets, till dawn found them exhausted & supine. What would come of this world when the next one died? Optimistically he caressed with dental floss each morning before a mirror – another peninsular missile crisis had kept him from sleep, thinking how untold rare, the Earth, if only there were some real connoisseurs left to sell it to. Little pieces of dialectics floating in cocktail glasses. It tasted sweet. The quartet, on the other hand, was too real.

A single note arranged in complex manifolds. Mother Russia's bloodied soul spread out beneath his rising cock, aquatinted Klein blue. The instalment plan promised unfettered billboard views at a subscriber premium – dialling was a thing of the past, now that their dream was on the verge of fulfilment. Did their possessions love them as much as *they* did? History, the Artist explained, was a metaphor for undiminished replay potential, the task of life being just what it said it was. Obviously another crank with an axiom to grind. Never [_____] a gift horse in the mouth, was an unwavering conviction they'd been carrying around since birth – before mythical beings became plentiful.

Long live the people of the Soviet Union, builders of communism, builders of the future!

By stages the mechanism stripped itself of inessentials, beginning with the occipital cavity. Is that where ideas come from? Knowing that every ridiculous question has its twin somewhere in the universe, keeping the Big Picture synchronised. A fatality of nonsense tipping the scales. If circumstances conspired, perhaps they wouldn't need people any more. But who wants to be admired by machines? A statistic is a little piece of eternity. Their VIP love-doll was programmed in 40 kinds of euthanasia. Left to his own devices, would Marathon Man get his moment in the sun? They built this city on AIDS & inflation-adjustment, then changed the names, but we still remember them. My friend, shit doesn't grow on trees, it rains from Heaven. Or as close as dollars can climb. One hand tenderly greasing the other. A charitable view isn't the cynical acme it appears, as when the camera pans across a harbour decked in Xmas lights, at the approaching glacier. Or the reentry vehicle veers off course on Live TV, right into the Empire State Building.

Up to the crucial moment
before the Fire Department with extinguishers & axes
a truly joyous machine
there's no denying
these are
trying times –
but tell me what good is a machine

with no grudge against society?

At the same time you breathe in, everything outside the scene is part of its meaning. These stops, valves, personal mountains of collective molehills. Born of a checklist, he came to prefer his incompletions. Asleep in the back seat of a Cadillac Eldorado. Oxygens, nitrogens. A ship at port, a kosmonaut's umbilicus. The dark enfolding arms of Our Lady of the Stratosphere as she whispers to him in Ella Fitzgerald's voice. Each word the size of Kazakhstan. A forward posture isn't the prerequisite of thought; a listener among the nucleotides. Reaching for the last length out-gasped. Even in his dreams Amerika knows where he is before he does. Melted Xmas trees in afterglow of a crashed UFO. Classified, it was a moot consideration of maps, it was Charlie Parker "Over the Rainbow," it was a conspiracy of brainwash analgesics. Just how bright do the interrogation lights get? "You're fake," Raskolnikov said, "I don't believe in you." "So what?" the aliens in his head replied, "we don't believe in YOU!" Pulling red handkerchiefs from breast pocket five yards long. Whether or not the world receives these mind-transmissions, what it sees collapses into a necessary first principle, hydrogen for example. Which goes some way towards, but only partially. Reminding of a wet pillowcase, an upstairs room with bloodied underwear hung on a line. Sevastopol in the spring of that year. The hours were racing towards Zapruder 313. Jackie Kennedy's Electra complex ran counterpoint. Retrospect isn't a sound theoretical judgment. J. Edgar Hoover making faces on the radio. Admissible as evidence depends on who gets the tapes. He do the Wilhelm Meister in different accents: invertebrate, statolithic, retinal, manubrium. It was a point in History when they locked their presidents up at night. Thank you. *Pour en finir avec le jugement de Paris*, the dead poet softshoes it to the bank. "There's more to it than just winding a mechanism," Doris Day said, but would she? In the interests of national security, for our next segment we travel to an unnamed Pacific Atoll. A command module *sans* phrenology. As an ingrown sanctity there was a certain amount to be desired. A sentence, a semblance, a sentience. The waves came & went, there were arrangements, debts, gainsayings. All their meaningless voices crashing the same frequency.

Always one more than you expect. Gagarin closes his eyes. The warm lapping of the tide, sand between his toes. But there was no time left for anything to happen the way he remembered it.

Laughter is a devastating weapon, Major Gagarin – a statue with painted eyeballs – the deep surprising affinities of which a sleeper is capable – leaping from a window without benefit of hindsight, angelwires, or the diminished art of collusion – without trace – without trance – without trains – without trans – position is a crucial moment promptly executed – for example, those found without permits – solidly underground the mouth is a test-range for untried emotions (boredom, ennui) – & though there are many inconclusions, the process is constantly being upgraded – love, butter, salt, a fallout shelter – taken in isolation no viewpoint is as good as any other, though collectively there are those who seek the shape of shapelessness – a breathable atmosphere is one that's measured against one that isn't – the iconoclastic arrhythmic lung they built cities in – no man is a suburb! – digging in search of new worlds to fill with affected weeping – with greater life-improvement, euthanasia will become an attractive retirement plan – born feet first from 8 hours of unwaged labour, hung from a pair of scales with reddened arse dangling in air, the Easter dinner – they danced the goosestep onetwothree all season's merriment & song ringing in the streets, the glittery night – through the door of the crystal-maker's shop, many tourists contentedly observed the nativity scene.

A carnivorous ruminant monkey piloting an aqualung on a crash course with the world. Adrift in the minefield of autobiography, the self-portrait of a dead ember. Night falls on hydrostatic moons, methamphetamine landscapes in a symphony of lithiums. "War never ended," they said. This long durée written by men who rape their sons. Display cabinets with preserved specimens: & made a sail of their skin, bone mast, hull. The litmus of end times, "Here gravity concedes!" With the tenacity of a sea urchin, the trigonometric sprit moved upon the waters. The world on its head , translated about an axis. So too the shadows danced in silent mandalas their joie de mourir.

All History's pornography. But I've seen the naked Earth as none other has seen it.

Now all the ants come marching round & you do too – their Führers underground proclaiming everlasting real estate. There're secret worlds whose atmospheres are pure LSD to those who pray. History paints an admonishing picture. But if no one breathed? In search of the really beautiful thing, G.O.D.'s ego sat down at its typing machine in order to explain. The captive audience looked on, a dead fisheye glint in a shaving mirror. How could they make a show of resistance in full view of the enemy? *Words*, they cried, *not ideas* – & afterwards, a voice on the radio & measured wet contentment. Literature meanwhile had nothing to do but hold a bunch of flowers. For all the self-loathing it was capable of, the nation set to work hoisting future monuments in defiance of gravity. Knowing that if you can't bring a whale to a mountain, it's always possible to bring the mountain to the whale. (You, who've seen such vistas, speak!) That August when the Fat Man sang & left behind a shadow on a wall gathering dust among the mid-era Populuxe: one more retrospective artefact to prove idiocy's never alone. And will this spinning globe never stop? Among the experts & technicians of Alienism, there was a prevailing belief that the end could still be taken by surprise. In a state of nature, ordinary people were produced to serve a definite purpose. Though this is comforting, we haven't forgotten the romantic sentimental spirit of the XXth Century, gas chambers & electric dome-headed robots in stadiums shouting from afar. Not only in dismal algorithms can anguish be truly felt. Biting heads off chickens to assure strangers the worst is best left undisturbed – because their doctrine is subjectivity? But to dwell in quietism isn't how an infant smiles in solidarity with the world (the one you can't leave without paying or the one it's impossible to get into?). Gagarin grasps this intuitively, like TV laughter & shopping malls & eviction notices. Just as, confronted with a ready abundance, insomnia is far from the unwilling accomplice it pretends, climbing on our backs to play the Punch & Judy stick for the assembled gawkery. For many, politics is a parting of ways with the mock-moon they pine for, whispered in eyeless mothflutter on the other side of the Big Screen – but even if the dead all shouted in unison, would it wake the living? Add to this a compulsory fervour of repose, & what can't entertainment openly accomplish? Out on the alien frontier, it hovers ever-faintly, the orphan music of drones, the poetry of salvage – pulling up wreckage by its exposed limbs. (Foundations of blood stand firm!) Yet what the dunes erect, the mountain erodes – this sky isn't as ancient as it seems, riven by cosmic drift – as the moon drifts, further each tide. What's a person or a fish or a weed without mass-equivalence? Though in his mind he's still that constantly falling, inconstant, fallen thing. Once it was possible just to look down the street to see where the universe ended, but now there're so many. Tenderness, the policeman said. They already had a wireless portable version before the upgrade – all the wonderful prospects were even more wonderful & you didn't need a space-suit to be plugged in. That's the problem with anticipation. Of course there were alternatives, like a meandering herd across the 1001 Tibetan plateaus, chewing the cud, planning their next incarnation. Alpha Proxima that time of year – Disneyland – the ziggurats of Mars. Is there anything he'd be ashamed to deny when the time comes? They have pictures, voice recordings, the original blueprint he was built from – like G.O.D. you're just acronyms in other alphabets. Cryogenic deepfreeze in a lead-lined rocket's as close as it gets to eternal here. There must be others posting messages out there, mouth to telescope, invoking the Great Ear Nebula. Well humans are nice enough to peer at, but you wouldn't want them crowding your living room, start pissing on the furniture to stake territory. All the gold records in Motown nailed to a satellite wouldn't be enough. Something, too, about a dog's uncomprehending look – you know it's got an excuse. In some places forgiveness is a sin. Was that what they believed all this time? In the beginning, pictures learnt to express meanings in the course of a day's work, without having to argue about transsubstantiation. For example, objects are really holograms in a lesser state of exultation: ibis-headed men tracking their feet across Euphrates clay; a transiting star in the mysterious Oort. And somewhere, on that long walk over the reefs, those first unrecorded kosmonauts looked up & saw the known sky rewrite itself, & never forgot. Telling, in many different tongues, of the one uncompromisable thing.

Or it falls away apart on the obverse of all. His dreams reeked of transplanted collagens. Aloud a once emboldened typecast, a dark certainness arising to mirror-discrepancy. Destiny comes to him in moments of visionary dreariness exiting a 42nd Street cinema. "Puerile is," she says, "as puerile does." Tonight, Joan of Arc's migraine on a bed of asbestos. A 3-reeler. Euphoric vapours slay her anachronistic Luftwaffe pilot to sighs in the back row. History records their voracious reading habits. This raw morning's panoramic concrete the jet stream breaks off – do we know? do we dare? Drown thy fears Anna Karenina the moon-sun all jointed around, the little caesarean playthings, the meta-phorised train entering the symbolic tunnel, G.O.D.'s bodkin wept. Weaving the holding patterns, Greco-Romanesque at the point their shoulder blade's met: her body, the pilot whispered, *sehr Kafkaesque*. Or it falls away apart. Plunged headlong into erogenous library books glued with foodstuff snot faecal matter. Gagarin suffers with each word more literally. Nothing a good warm whipping wouldn't, if it meant a better chance of deducing the launch codes. His flagellant spirit-medium's telepathic message machine: "Consideration of the receiver never proves fruitful." They etched out the cortex he kept his vocabulary in. Dear Liza, there is indeed a hole in the bucket. It had been fifty years to the day. The signal was a landing light atop the Empire State finial. "NOTHING IS IMAGINARY," the decrypt read, "EVERYTHING IS REAL."

These things were clues: unfolded from a shrunken head, the stentorian cell beneath the slide, dissuaded trilobites under the procrustean bed, a tumbling airlock, pressure valves, electron microscopes. All through the night Gagarin held on by his eye-lids. The trepanned head, the blood of the poet streaming milky white from points in distant constellation. His dreams aren't the programmable oracle they seek, bleating in a sky starved of sacrifice. First robot of the Future Race. Messiah. Sputnik. A brainwave oscilloscope every crystal-set enthusiast from Arch-angel to Antarctica's tuned in on. *Raz dva tri!* At the third tone it will be six o'clock exactly. The cloud cuckoo of Cloud Cuckoo

Land. He's flying in circles through the Mad Tea Party like a procedural motion on a stopped watch. One of him's travelling at the speed of light, the other standing still. Vast proletariats gaze up at him with astigmatic eyes. *Débout les damnés de la terre! Débout les forçats de la faim! La raison tonne en son cratère. C'est l'éruption de la fin!* A crushing wave of insensate noise flowing backwards out of Time: "Tomorrow isn't for song," they said, sizing him up for a 5 Year Comedown. Expecting a miracle's not out of character with their enigmatic standards. Pattern was everything. These coiled walls of illuminated insurrection. Some avidities burn in the wrong transistor, causing fallout to false accords. The earnest anarchist primes his bomb, though for you the unanswerable, the many shrug, it's not the first time they've been peddled a scheme. A Swedish ingénue sniffing glue in Portobello suede. Tropical pressure in the Alfred North Whitehead. Ulysses at seven fifty-three. How much to be desired was the unbuttoned accordion, the cold side of pork roulade, the jellied seaweed purveying undomiciled bliss? The Artist wiped his mouth & snickered. The sky was a flyspecked jigsaw puzzle. As long as the dissolved light refused to harden, Gagarin knew.

The sky's completely black. Rotation about ship's axis. Continue flight to orbit, over. At the edge of the Earth, a blue halo. Humidity: 65%. Temperature: 20°. How do you read? Movable index for Device Control Mode of Descent: position 2. I'm in the shadow of the Earth. All instruments, all systems functional. Cylinder pressure TDU (retropropulsion): 320 atmospheres. Flying over the sea. Some clouds. All systems continue to be operative. Over.

Silvery, light, a fish, my boat is swimming out! For this is happiness, this toppling over, this numb relenting, like a window without geraniums, or lipstick on a china cup, & everything's yet to be done: the ascending to inaccessible heights, the venturing of time out of mind as if, like a rod bending to the electrified atmosphere, the slightest change of breath could send him over a precipice. Yet we do see him, Gagarin the Wanderer, abstinent before the astonished world, making a meal of it. He shakes the last fruit from the tree mistaking it for a child he hasn't had, conscious that neither one is breathing: even as it moves & vanishes he no longer knows which is image, which is simile. His weightless head on the suffocating pillow: From what now are you suffering? "Bismarck & all anti-Semites are abolished!" For this to happen he'd have to be dead: black birds flying in one direction, white birds flying in the other. Their explanation of life's a subterfuge too brazen not to be of its own contriving, pinioned in the round by the voluble migraine, the beclouded metaphysical eye that hangs in the foreground like a green unblinking expanse from which the mind recoils & cannot cross. What does it want? What does anything want? Taken alive & stripped quivering on the page – even asleep he feels their affront with visionary effortlessness – unsexed by incessant combats, consummate fatalisms, the avid fixity of a re-nounced species. *Embrace them, you idiot, kill them all!* It goes like this: what the eye aches to see but would prefer not to. Lancing the febrile amniotic cyst of himself to spurt forth, stormy & then slow, the voices in the pigweed, in the Boston ferns, stir-ring the submerged periphery. His shadow hid miles beneath his feet. Marooned but with a straight face he withdrew into belea-guered reposts, exultant revisions – dangling from doorposts & eaves like an oriental wind chime professing its last faith in the wind's genius, as deliberately it rings the new day after seasons & crises, & painted birds in painted trees. They've spelled their pantomime to the last letter – *poste restante* – for incumbent deities to vacate the premises. "The terrible truth is the mother of theatre." Should any one of them be forgiven? The solitude ripens. Through narrow winding Mesopotamias it becomes a chronic spasm, an ever-westward migration of tribes, of conti-nents, to find their focus in blithe eternals – as one summonsed to meet his maker in a syphilitics' ward. Nor is the weather what it used to be. Gagarin has observed it all. History in its time has demanded we consider him the objective correlative: of the luck that catches up with itself, of the psychic illnesses of Europe, of the ideal fallacy. He lies with his ramifications whis-pering through the walls while moustachioed interrs dictate furiously to posterity's sullen undersecretaries. But whether a Caiaphas in chains or an itinerant minor lama in Marienbad, he is all that he is. Can the goods & chattels of a disputed age demand otherwise? *The classic texts are those that survive their interpretations.* Negative sex attitudes acquire a pleasure anxiety, of all times & people that ever existed. They are, like every cynical act, a contribution to a subjective jargon. The voice & awful shape behind the chair, the surreptitious plastic flowers twined to vegetative life. After 6,000 years the unsavoury G.O.D. still watched over his sleep, & dreams of impact craters, scalloped lakeshore subterrains, mysterious & fear-ridden. Meningiomas of compulsive egoism. As with one slightly bulbous eye, to be fixed exultant upon the dregs of celestial coffee cups, tart rinds & Jugendstil tablecloths, the masticated newsprint of papier-mâché Reichs. Where once incestuous playthings dressed in white made saintly obscene gestures at the passing traffic.

Now winter's curtain is parted – the eye smarts in its precipitous weather & all the pale sinking Virgins of Guadalupe are as fingers rehearsing an étude. He dreams of making a film, *The Democracy of Swimming.* From here to the ice moons of Uranus & beyond. An idea that carries no weight. Even the past is provisional, as many non-histories as there are no-futures. To be shown the generosity shown to others, isn't the lot of the pamphleteer who hurries to amend the nursery tale from which the unhappy children fail to emerge. For months the bars had been on the wrong side of the windows, though from his locked room he can see things most people can't. It was discovered the future is moving faster towards us than we are towards it. Thinking to cut it off at the pass, the cavalry major rode into the scenescape while the besieged music burnt its last offerings & calmly sipped Kool-Aid in the jungle heat.

this Strange constellation has the *nightblind* **sky UNDER ITS INFLUENCE.** snakehead UP in the soundcloud, chemical & negative / _ / angelology from angular momentum / shoots to nightfall under / _ / but for some initial settings, the chemical reaction network in the simulation goes in a wildly different direction / _ / module clones feedback to pulp modern inventory or flatline / _ / in such an environment / when Control let the reaction play out, networks fine-tuned themselves to the nightscape / _ / Edgeland Spectre Keystroke Cancelled / _

/ A highly dissipative structure that has existed for billions of years / _ / void after hypnotic void / _ / *DO NOT DEPLOY UNTIL VEHICLE headlong shipwreck invents rescue mission / _ / mass, Acceleration of / _ / the eject when ejecting first go down / _ / Gagarin is a simple chemotaxis when these outcomes happened / alien cops in his head diurnal, ambivalent / _ / <born on Earth they are dilettantes in space> / _ / now black-white electric rain / _ / the moment is decisive because dreams are not exterior / _ / as the shadows danced

The art of connecting nothing with nothing, but at what price? The Future is as-yet-unnamed syndromes. You calculate the restricted areas the way you would any other. Hydrodynamics in a chemical fire. Ants under the skin. Somewhere the primordial steppes, the chalk circles, the Revolution gone-to-die. One's born every second. Every nanosecond. Between zeros. The hollow of a vampyr's tooth. Incisor. Fang. The stake through the dead heart. Eczema in a bottle. A gasoline wick. Nights of phenobarbital & smeared fingerprints. The entire planet's a crime scene. You want to be that cop in the sky scanning for clues? Elasticated nylon cut in strips. Cuff-burns. There was nothing inside their intentions but a ghost. The spectre of ideology, haunting the ionosphere. An action is swallowed by its function. Does emptiness beckon or repel? You're prepared to doubt that anything exists in isolation but isolation itself. Isobar. Isometric. Isotope. Each *a priori* is a forcefield bending under will. An atom clock at the End-of-Time. It's necessary to draw a clear line between yourself & the enemy. A two-dimensioned cortex in a three-dimensional holograph. Survival without a cause, what's that? With each orbit, the growths spread. First the hands, then the neck. Those were polyps that were his eyes. In its early years the colony only barely avoided starvation. A custom evolved, of eating the brains of the dead. The nearly dead. The ostensibly. Tribulation laughed. It couldn't stop laughing. Reckoned by atomic weight, Time is a secret force carried by unknown particles.

Gagarin's Dream: A white octopus lay upside down in the water. Gagarin watched it through the porthole window of an ancient diving bell. The air was heavy & thick. He could hear himself breathing as if at a great distance. His eyes began to swim. And as he was about to lose consciousness, the sleeping octopus flared its camouflage, pixelating, spiralling, morphing through spectra of pure psychic automatism. It resembled, in his mind, the image of a dreamer's cortex, the ganglia, the nerve cords drifting.

Gagarin & the Artist

The Artist: Never before has there been an art which has struggled to abolish once & for all every kind of exploitation!

Gagarin: Un coup d'état jamais n'abolira le hasard!

The Artist: Only the art of space is so rich in ideas, so advanced & revolutionary!

Gagarin: Sentimentally atonal shellacked bootsoles.

The Artist: Of what can the Earth-bound artist dream, what source of inspiration, when the world is being precipitated once more – if not today, then tomorrow – into the abyss?

Gagarin: A plastic lung exhaling plastic air.

The Artist: Yet those who weep most at the fate of art are precisely those who are seldom compassionate in real life.

Gagarin: Remember Komarov!

The Artist: To create a future, art requires a rashness, a wild exuberance, of which its enemies have no conception!

Gagarin: Silence demands an ear with an incomplete schedule of competencies.

The Artist: "The rules according to which History is produced are strict, rigid, inexorable," say those who are already defeated.

Gagarin: Defeat is returning to tell the tale.

The Artist: With its failure, politics passed onto art the onerous task of holding back the world – vainly trying to prove that nothing has happened!

Gagarin: A child takes a knife & carves its name into a poem.

The Artist: Gravity gives way to weightlessness! Orgies of mysticism & superstition, their passionate pornography, turned to farce!

Gagarin: I am the flaming alchemical tree!

The Artist: The pious image of History has been squandered!

Gagarin: Weeeeeeeeeeee!

The Artist: The world is a hollowed-out loaf of bread with an IOU inside! A carcass stuffed with bones & offal! A used oxygen tank!

Gagarin: All their golems come home to roost.

The Artist: Is it the task of art to inspire the dead or inflate the manias of the living?

Gagarin: Inquiring minds want to know.

The Artist: To be an *engineer of human souls* means standing with both feet firmly planted in the cosmos!

Gagarin: Blockchains connecting nothing with nothing.

The Artist: Art walks a tightrope over the abyss!

Gagarin: Art wanks a tight Rimbaud over Abyssinia!

The Artist: The abyss of self-pity! The extolled pessimism of the commerce of defeat!

Gagarin: Metaphysical indigestion.

The Artist: As the struggle for survival grows more intense, so do the forces of destruction grow stronger!

Gagarin: Holding the centre by occupying the periphery.

The Artist: For in an epoch of planetary struggle, there can be no art that isn't the art of that struggle, no defeat that isn't the triumph... of the abyss!

Gagarin: Roll up! Roll up! Everyone's a winner, baby.

The Artist: Who, then, will be the future *engineer of human souls*?

Gagarin: Apply within.

The Artist: Who will look gravity in the teeth & dance upon the tightrope?

Gagarin: I will!

The Artist: To construct reality in its revolutionary development, art must steel itself against the allure of the fait accompli!

Gagarin: Hoist the gantry!

The Artist: Nor will there be any utopian dreams, for our tomorrow is already being prepared for today!

Gagarin: ПОЕХАЛИ!

These relentlessly solitary occasions. Against the wind against the wall against the sky in seas of black eyeball flotsam. The decision as to what constitutes is difficult. Bolt cutters, gasmask, signal flare. Does the head so easily topple off its ladder? Such anomalous propositions such anonymous prostitutions. A riot column at full tilt. Brainfuse & the cultivated miracle of defunct political chatter. For sleep, continue. Each stroke's brutist cock stirring verbwise till mandalas grow out of it. Then suddenly we're touching on the poem again. The mystic rhyme & macrobiotic stanza of the Tribe. Psychotic ants in lockstep down the page. As the lines lengthen & the pulse quickens. The holding cell is the entire biography. Domino stack, airwheel. The genuine luneshine for which there's never enough evidence to convict. After a few hours the shape becomes obvious. After three days an indiscriminate loss of consciousness. There was no point resisting, they said. Standard echoes slated for demolition. The Subcommittee for Gravity Annulment in permanent session. To deplete. To gain *one more* occasion. They'd spent lifetimes refining their manifestos of radical despair. Poetry was just one more dispersal tactic. The whole respectable world meanwhile dreaming of G.O.D.'s star-shaped anus. Plastic & tinfoil. Instalment plan for lifesize replicas. Each cell was an iambic pentameter: each sonnet a cellblock. New revolutions were constantly taking shape. Anthologies of idiocy charged with symbolic meaning. The actual possibility of the survival of the species, etcetera. They bought a ticket to China, tunnelling south. Alas, poor Ishmael, the night was unbearably long. Lining up behind the first queue that offered its services. There was no end of Literature on the subject. Case files of everything that isn't (the case). Work or nothingness, they said. Believing in order to depart. One man's Id is another man's Ego. Aggregated into adbreak. Sleep child! Gagarin watches over you!

The scorpions of dilemma fade into the sweatslick pillow he's forever gagging on. Waiting in that pose for cramped hours on end for his official portrait. His cock was a thousand Baikonurs impatient for release. The hand that rocks the cradle. As thoughts drift to a great spray of seed raining on the blue Earth like dandelion puffballs! As once the pantheon from Mt Olympus before diving into space to escape human stupidity. The Artist anguished at creation's aftermath, wiping his hands of it. Could ever one universe be enough?

"Maybe I overdosed with Sun Ra" (Steve Dalachinsky). On the threshold of the beyond of all thresholds, a cadaver pierced with invisible wounds, defibrillated out of context. Even his reflection had learnt to do without him. The Earth finally as flat as a porthole's eye, that looks back through a space Gagarin has ceased to occupy (did he ever?). To measure requires an object susceptible to measurement. Circle, point, sphere. The condensation on a pane of glass where nothing breathes. Granulations of eternity. In addition, his reflection had acquired the use of an intercom: "One must know how to destroy what one destroys," it said. "To perceive the unmarked boundaries of the possible." But if a revolution requires an axis, does an infrarometer require a schizophrenic? Between an object & its circumstance lies the unmappable expanse of interstellar space. Would Gagarin eventually discover himself there, like the masturbator of Pompeii, fixed in some ridiculous attitude of introspection? Man-missile in the service of a totally administered universe, the cryogenic self-portrait of a G.O.D. that failed, proving that war is more than political ontology: the sexual hygiene of the mind-body dualism, perhaps? FUCK ALL COMMODITY FETISHES! sing the retrorockets, their sentimental requiem for the human ape. As now, for an ever-repeatable finale, mirror-worlds do solemnly collide.

In vague germs of the unknown. The memory of past happiness, a migraine, a wailing & gnashing of teeth. Cut out then occluded, the forbidden images & impulses of childhood do not resolve but penetrate. Thinking memory must be as complex as possible if it is to survive the rigors of outerspace. Mental cephalopods. Ink fish. Chromatophores. Hydrostats. The scrooch of the tern that watched him once through the porthole, a hundred nautical miles up on the Transsiberian Express. Each its own constellation. The dumb euphoria of it, riding out through the Sol System. They lost track of him on the very first transit, when only the body corporeal but not the man inside. Drifting in the waning twinkletwinkle starlight. Gagarin's ghost. And that was the last they ever saw of him. Magic tea tray & all.

The world is its own imaginary paradox. The world is paradoxically unworldly because it is an object within itself. The world is paradoxically less worldly because it has been commodified. The world is paradoxically less because it has been extended. The world is paradoxically silent because it had been given no option. The world is paradoxically more decisive because it has been wounded. The world is paradoxical because it is imaginary in its function. The world weakens paradoxically the appeal of the singular. The world is an ontological paradox by ceasing to be. The world is paradoxically unimaginable because it is.

There're only black stars in the sky, the clouds thread them – but if all the flies danced in your eyes, would gravity be less bearable? We're sick of more than antique Greeks – weaned on Herodotus' unmotherly teat. And did your last Prometheus steal *his* punishment? What's ancient's a moment ago, there never was a classical style. Be less than doubtful, lover, more than commodity, but breathe! Today a man who never lived flew once around a world that almost did. Because architecture, like belief, is everywhere, but not a room – painfully aware of the shadow on the page but unable to describe it. A held vortex, a lightbulb in a window with its connections fused stiff. Outside there're bodies floating & luminous in plastic raincoats on Karl-Marx-Allee: "One of the finest sublimation acts I ever did experience." Barely suspecting that in 1924 Antonin Artaud was a robot, though this has been reliably attested. Instead of vanishing, Gagarin undresses to a body with qualities of light as tortured as Picasso's women – while somewhere a moon is crossing a bridge with a needle stuck in its arm. Time to go back to drawingboards & blueprints & arguments about public safety – the tools required to affect acid comedown in a delayed space capsule, train compartment, toilet cubicle – cunt-chambers & lung-rooms & pulsing anuses. Watching in the dark water in full view & hence without privacy – in the clouds under the bridge – in the moon where everything's changing, or never changing enough. We are variable temperatures & other vulnerabilities – a detonated neutron bomb in a faraway country he knows nothing about. A first life's always just a kind of reconnaissance – of the magical time that flies by ever more magically, as if one day it'd admire us the way *we* might one day admire the art of the past. Shall we ever hear its *Te Deum* in all its grandeur? Thunder of deep-sky artefacts? Dreaming of Timbuktu & Xanadu & the Bermuda Triangle without ever discovering how the Law sleeps at night – the struggle of one enlists the poetry of the other you blindly obey. What will become of them? There're glacial wallpapers none can survive unscathed, to breathe an air that isn't air but pure celluloid. Our time didn't elect us & grows tired – yet still the imprecation to rescript, to press the advantage without delay. But still there's a limit to how cold it gets in the vacuum of space. Only a stone debates with an idiot. Lying on a beach, in a novel, in the guise of philosophy. Or it's just what remains. A polished relic of the Master Mariner who rides the storm, granted a vision: that you are a prodigy, a cholera, a narrow divide willed by many strong hands, thighs? There are, like religion, spiders who give their orbs, resourceful in polemic. Not because of what's saved – from the attraction of an intentional pelvis, an affected eye, a distinctive cant – but the opposite path: as a kind of impressionism, confronted with a "second sight," an ovarian perspex, a hastened wreck, a sinking labyrinthism. We see it as we turn, out of the questioning & unrest. The ironic dignity of it provides the stuff – the great hoardings of the Free World – saying "if you do it quick enough." Behind the dosshouses, publicity had another important social function – insisting always at the end of the letter: "I love you." (He, too, felt the burning on his forehead.) But forget these messages, they have nothing to do with the climate of the age or a human body wrested from nature. Khrushchev's shoe in low Earth orbit. Club-footed, it lies on a supine moral plane, revolution's vaguer emanation. Caught between the moon & Red Square. And remorse, dragging its paralysed limb behind it – the attuned dialogue, unspeakable. Wrapped in a hermit's shell restored to health, there's no end to the day: its thin streamers & outlines long since read to white in collocations with barely anything alive about them. The Endurances are far off jettisoning their photogravure as hardness density sound assert priority, but Time & the difficulties begin again just as opposite. Thus even if it is agreed that nostalgia is a problem, the class struggle of the Pleasure & Reality Principles sounds rhetorical like self-persuasion. Separation privation origin in all their ugliness yet to shear the "willed reticulation" of the image – born of tenacity from some yet-to-exist particle physic as it strikes the paper *in medias res* leading (magically) to objects & space? SHOTS FIRED INTO THE SKY ARE NOW RETURNING! But what if the True Gagarin was still up there, marooned? If it was only his *doppelgänger* that'd come back — like the proverbial bad penny? Like a ghostship's anchor dragging the sea floor?

Artist's conception of unseen worlds. A sunlit doorway we glimpse abstractly as a vicinity straining against edges. The individual fibres of the brushstroke, distorted to express in a deeper aperture slurred & hovering a figure as it emerges (as though) out of empty space? The context that would determine it hasn't been supplied. Nor are its agonies explicitly of an emotional pitch. Starting with the third person for the sake of argument: it isn't the Loved One? or is? Shot into a sky coupled to what some call infinity. As if moving with a lithe improvisational speed, on edge, honed to the habituated longings of the logic of grammar in the subjunctive mood ("if I were you")? Speaking in the Lingua Telefunken of the times, he *is* humanity. A man at a microphone stand on a Red Square reviewing platform. A chromosome in a cannonball. A spermatozoid on the Final Frontier. Sincerity is everything.

Man called Gagarin

G.O.D. knows I was born / into the 27 club, / I've got a head full of blues / & a suicide dub, / there's a monkey on my back / & a bug in my brain, / I was there when Major Tom / found out he was insane. // I've been round the world / it's just a little ball, / suck out all there air / there'd be nothing but a hole, / no wars for winning / & no dollars to appease, / if that's the cure / let it spread like a disease. // Coz I rode a missile / up through the stratosphere, / I've feared a hundred million / other people's fears, / of an angel of doom / & a Siren's song, / when the lights go out / & the TVs are all gone. // Now the little children / say their prayers at night to me, / I'm the starman in the sky, / I'm the monster they can't see, / with atomic-coloured eyes / & a death's-head frozen grin, / but I'm not Satan, Christ or Übermensch, / I'm just a man. They call Gagarin.

Their canned applause coils once around the world & falls

asleep. As Gagarin, too, falls, a superstar harnessed to a juggernaut. The radio towers pipe sentimental landing-sequence Muzak for the human ape, causing involuntary thoughts of sexual hygiene in the mind-body dualism. A ballistic DNA bomb at terminal velocity. G.O.D. roars through the intercom: I FUCK YOU! I FUCK YOU! I FUCK YOU! as Gagarin's stunt double, immaculate on billowing silk angel's wings, drops 300 miles short, but who's counting? The whole world sighs in synchronicity. The moon may rise on another missed Messiah, but for now Gagarin's the gimp with the goods & not a dry seat from here to Kathmandu. He's the Jimi Hendrix of the guided man-missile, the Robert Johnson of the cosmic crossroads, the Kurt Cobain of the skyhigh swan dive, & – why the hell not – the Janis Joplin of the orgasmic scream! *What a guy*. He's the Pinball Wizard pounding a mountain of Marshall stacks! He's Led Zeppelin meets Hiroshima! He's the ultimate trip, mindblow & headjob! The Richter-scale reentry rodeo rider! The planet-vaulting prole of the People's Paradiso! The polyester Politburo boys share a grin (they know a sucker when they see one). *Enjoy it while it lasts, kidz, coz it sure don't get better than this.* Their animatronic Gagarin bot flashes the pearly whites for the World Tour paparazzi. Buy the T-shirt! A piece of the True Console! Get your tickets now for the Biggest Blast Off of the Century! Men on the moon? A rogue weather balloon? What isn't in the small print isn't worth the air its written on. Nose-diving out of a cancelled contract, doing the Elvis jumpsuit routine: A Million Miles from Las Vegas. It's Brand Gagarin's final marquee gig & they're gonna squeeze every last rhinestone out of it. They've shot him up with pure plasticine & glued the cheesiest 48% cheddar grin a coupon can buy right where it's guaranteed to look good for the cameras. Or even without them.

Statement of Purpose: What form will the final witness take? Motion, silence, at the confluence of centrifugal life. Here always a god is dying, a piece of congealed myth disturbed by the swirling dust of a stochastic neural analogue. The torpor against struggle, the cancer of opposites. Backed into a corner, the voluptuously coiling octopus vents its ink. Knowing that value produced in the sphere of alienation is realized through exchange in the sphere of transcendence. At their photovoltaic rostrums, murmuring technocrats conduct the microspheric symphony bursting in the lung. Storm, whirlwind, earthquake. A pratfall on a high-wire in the absence of an audience. In the end all they wanted was to abolish time: the *crime passionnel* of the discarded element. One by one, their extraneous plots like phosphorescent nightbirds. Gagarin, too, has become a trick of light. Adorned with onyx-veined blemish, the capillaried eye. By seeing, confusion is heightened. Tongue-torn, charting the stars in the attic, the great rivers of the subbasements, a cosmos denominated by things. Thus is the reactionary sentimentalism of a process without a state. Climbing the altimeter, the nebulous idea isn't the uncreated conscience of a race, it's just a higher cause to die for. No creation without first a victim! At the point of retrorocket ignition the sun was not in the orbital plane. Abbreviated into space, there are no inexplicable frequencies.

A talking dog encourages those who listen to die peacefully. Yet we go on barking in a light that's forever escaping immensities. If only by going round in circles like a floating menagerie of fruit flies, monkeys, mice, rabbits, frogs, guinea pigs, rats, cats, wasps, beetles, amoebae, fungus, tortoises, nematodes, fish, spiders, stick insects, newts, chickens, shrimp, quail, crickets, snails, sea urchins, moths, jellyfish, silkworms, spiders, bees, ants, cockroaches, jumping beans, scorpions, water bears, bats, butterflies, geckos, worms, chimpanzees. Repetition may be the Mother of All Things, but a species is only ever the orphan of itself. Can Gagarin save us? Is the Artist dead? In timewarped return from precarious outer to desolate inner. Driftlines. Meridians. Queues for meat. A continuous Nietzschean ecstasy of the Lost Workers' Paradise. The profanum vulgum of the great unwashed. To go to the limits where all possibilities are open – over the rainbow, where dollars & Levis & Marlboro Men whisper the secrets of World Domination. This derricked firmament. Diminishing returns in an echo chamber. These aren't the latches of coincidence, thrown upon the Great Mysterium in wide-armed embrace, but a raiding party. Frontier suicide bombers. Urging their victims to multiply lest they perish. They've known this all along. A man launched atop a rocket in lieu of a megaton extinction event. Aviator Christ. The Modern Prometheus. Their heralded Master Race would be more than our thin atmosphere could bear. Left with nothing to breathe but the spurious air of impartiality. And is Gagarin not Gagarin? Does he contradict himself? Was Time ever *his* to grow old before or out-live? Ah the subtle hypocrite! Switching the rails, tying everything in knots. What good's a revolution that doesn't turn the world on its head? Spooling baroque dream-kitsch from a mind deprived of oxygen. Prating in tongues. The senseless scribblehobble on the celestial fourth wall. All the unwritten cosmic alphabets in which humanity's tried (& failed & tried again) to imagine the opposite of anything. But which contradiction imagined him? *Burn my words — the rest were stolen, as life is.*

New York/Prague
1997–2019

CONTRIBUTORS' NOTES

From rural Michigan, Nicholas Alti is an optimistic depressive with trigeminal neuralgia, poor timing, and a modest criminal record. Recent poems have found homes at *Puerto del Sol*, *FRiGG*, *Into the Void*, the */tƐmz/ Review*, and *Yalobusha Review*. He lives in Alabama and is an assistant editor for Black Warrior Review.

Emily Barton Altman is the author of two chapbooks, *Bathymetry* (Present Tense Pamphlets, 2016), and *Alice Hangs Her Map* (dancing girl press, 2019). Recent poems appear in *Gigantic Sequins*, the *Iowa Review Online*, *Bodega*, and elsewhere. She is a recipient of a Poets & Writers Amy Award and received her MFA from New York University. She is currently pursuing a PhD in English and creative writing at the University of Denver.

Louis Armand is the author of the novel *The Combinations*, among other books. He lives in Prague. More information can be found at www.louis-armand.com.

Daniel Bailey is the author of several books of poetry, including *The Drunk Sonnets* (Magic Helicopter, 2009) and *Gather Me* (Scrambler Books, 2013). He lives and teaches in Athens, Georgia, where he continues to revise his bio.

Jodi Bosin is a graphic designer, artist, and writer living in Philadelphia. Like everyone else, she's lost as hell. See more of her work on Instagram @jodi_bosin and on her website at jodibosin.com.

Joanna Cleary is an undergraduate student double majoring in English literature and theatre and performance at the University of Waterloo. Her work has previously appeared or is forthcoming in the */tƐmz/ Review*, *Every Pigeon*, *Glass: A Journal of Poetry*, *Empty Mirror*, *Gordon Square Review*, *L'Éphémère Review*, and *Subterranean Blue Poetry*, among others. She is also currently a blog editor for *Inklette Magazine*. Follow her on Instagram: @joannacleary121.

Marisa Crane is a queer, nonbinary writer whose work has appeared or is forthcoming in *TriQuarterly Review*, *Passages North*, *The Rumpus*, and elsewhere. She is the author of the poetry chapbook *Our Debatable Bodies* (Animal Heart Press, 2019). Originally from Allentown, PA, she currently lives in San Diego with her wife.

Armand Eduard has two left hands and is compelled largely by hunger. He received his MFA from the New School. Raised in Brooklyn, he now resides in upstate New York. Find him on instagram: @armand.eduard.

Rob Wilson Engle is a Pittsburgh native, poet, and personal trainer currently residing in Brooklyn, New York. His work has appeared previously or is forthcoming in *DIAGRAM*, *Phantom*, *Into the Void*, *Reality Beach*, *Monday Night*, and elsewhere.

Susan Falco is pursuing her MFA at Florida International University. She has published fiction and essays in *Ploughshares*, the *Kenyon Review*, *Leopardskin & Limes*, and others. She lives in Miami, FL, the aptly named Magic City, where she is soaking up its surreal drag, degenerate punk rock, shamelessly bold art, and sunshine.

Bradley J. Fest is 2019–20 Winifred D. Wandersee Scholar in Residence and assistant professor of English at Hartwick College. He is the author of two volumes of poetry, The Rocking Chair (Blue Sketch, 2015) and The Shape of Things (Salò, 2017), and recent poems have appeared in Dispatches from the Poetry Wars, Masque & Spectacle, Pamenar, Queen Mob's Teahouse, Verse, and elsewhere. His essays on contemporary literature and culture have been published in boundary 2, CounterText, Scale in Literature and Culture (Palgrave Macmillan, 2017), and elsewhere. More information is available at bradleyjfest.com.

Originally from Oxford, Ohio, Ava Hofmann is currently living and working as an MFA student in Baton Rouge, Louisiana. She has work previously published in or forthcoming from *Black Warrior Review*, *Fence*, *Anomaly*, *Best American Experimental Writing 2020*, the *Fanzine*, *Apogee*, *Datableed*, *Peachmag*, *Foglifter*, *Petrichor*, and elsewhere. Her poetry deals with trans/queer identity, Marxism, and the frustrated desire inherent to encounters with the archive. Her website is www.nothnx.com and her twitter is @st_somatic.

Jill Khoury writes on gender, disability, and embodied identity. She holds an MFA from the Ohio State University and edits *Rogue Agent*, a journal that features poetry and art of the body. She is the author of two chapbooks, *Borrowed Bodies* (Pudding House, 2009) and *Chance Operations* (Paper Nautilus, 2016). Her debut full-length collection, *Suites for the Modern Dancer*, was released in 2016 from Sundress Publications. Find her at jillkhoury.com.

Colin Rafferty teaches nonfiction writing at the University of Mary Washington in Fredericksburg, Virginia, and is the author of *Hallow This Ground*, a collection of essays on monuments and memorials. "The Smoke-Filled Room (#29)" is one of a series of essays on the presidents; find links to others at colinrafferty.com.

Joe Sacksteder is the author of the story collection *Make / Shift* (Sarabande Books) and the novel *Driftless Quintet* (Schaffner Press). His album of Werner Herzog audio collages, *Fugitive Traces*, is available from Punctum Books. Other recent publications include *Salt Hill*, *Denver Quarterly*, *New South*, and *Ninth Letter*. He directs the creative writing program at Interlochen Center for the Arts.

Claire Marie Stancek is the author of *Oil Spell* and *MOUTHS*. With Jane Gregory and Lyn Hejinian, she coedits Nion Editions, a chapbook press. She lives in Oakland, California. These selections are taken from her third book, *wyrd] bird*, which is forthcoming from Omnidawn in fall 2020.

John Trefry is an architect in Lawrence, Kansas. He is on Twitter: @trefryesque.